THE BEDFORD SERIES IN HISTORY AND CULTURE

The German Reformation and the Peasants' War

A Brief History with Documents

Related Titles in
THE BEDFORD SERIES IN HISTORY AND CULTURE

Advisory Editors: Lynn Hunt, *University of California, Los Angeles*
David W. Blight, *Yale University*
Bonnie G. Smith, *Rutgers University*
Natalie Zemon Davis, *Princeton University*
Ernest R. May, *Harvard University*

Power and the Holy in the Age of the Investiture Conflict: A Brief History with Documents
Maureen C. Miller, *University of California, Berkeley*

Religious Transformations in the Early Modern World: A Brief History with Documents
Merry E. Wiesner-Hanks, *University of Wisconsin–Milwaukee*

UTOPIA by Sir Thomas More
Edited with an Introduction by David Harris Sacks, *Reed College*

The Saint Bartholomew's Day Massacre: A Brief History with Documents
Barbara B. Diefendorf, *Boston University*

The Enlightenment: A Brief History with Documents
Margaret C. Jacob, *University of California, Los Angeles*

England's Glorious Revolution, 1688–1689: A Brief History with Documents
Steven C. A. Pincus, *Yale University*

The French Revolution and Human Rights: A Brief Documentary History
Edited, Translated, and with an Introduction by Lynn Hunt, *University of California, Los Angeles*

DISCOURSE ON THE ORIGIN AND FOUNDATIONS OF INEQUALITY AMONG MEN by Jean-Jacques Rousseau with Related Documents
Edited with an Introduction by Helena Rosenblatt, *The Graduate Center, City University of New York*

THE BEDFORD SERIES IN HISTORY AND CULTURE

The German Reformation and the Peasants' War

A Brief History with Documents

Michael G. Baylor

Lehigh University

BEDFORD / ST. MARTIN'S   Boston ◆ New York

For Bedford/St. Martin's

Publisher for History: Mary Dougherty
Director of Development for History: Jane Knetzger
Executive Editor: Traci M. Crowell
Senior Editor: Heidi L. Hood
Developmental Editor: Ann Kirby-Payne
Editorial Assistant: Laura Kintz
Production Supervisor: Samuel Jones
Executive Marketing Manager: Jenna Bookin Barry
Project Management: Books By Design, Inc.
Text Design: Claire Seng-Niemoeller
Cover Design: Marine Miller
Cover Art: Peasant army on the march; woodcut from Johannes Stumpf, *Schweitzer Chronik* (Zurich, 1548), used with permission of the Zurich Zentralbibliothek.
Composition: Achorn International, Inc.
Printing and Binding: RR Donnelley and Sons

President: Joan E. Feinberg
Editorial Director: Denise B. Wydra
Director of Marketing: Karen R. Soeltz
Director of Production: Susan W. Brown
Associate Director, Editorial Production: Elise S. Kaiser
Manager, Publishing Services: Andrea Cava

Library of Congress Control Number: 2011941631

Manufactured in the United States of America.

7   6   5   4   3   2
f   e   d   c   b   a

For information, write: Bedford / St. Martin's, 75 Arlington Street, Boston, MA 02116 (617-399-4000)

ISBN: 978-0-312-43718-3

Acknowledgments

Acknowledgments and copyrights are continued at the back of the book on page 151, which constitutes an extension of the copyright page.

Distributed outside North America by PALGRAVE MACMILLAN
Houndmills, Basingstoke, Hampshire RG21 6XS

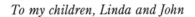

To my children, Linda and John

Foreword

The Bedford Series in History and Culture is designed so that readers can study the past as historians do.

The historian's first task is finding the evidence. Documents, letters, memoirs, interviews, pictures, movies, novels, or poems can provide facts and clues. Then the historian questions and compares the sources. There is more to do than in a courtroom, for hearsay evidence is welcome, and the historian is usually looking for answers beyond act and motive. Different views of an event may be as important as a single verdict. How a story is told may yield as much information as what it says.

Along the way the historian seeks help from other historians and perhaps from specialists in other disciplines. Finally, it is time to write, to decide on an interpretation and how to arrange the evidence for readers.

Each book in this series contains an important historical document or group of documents, each document a witness from the past and open to interpretation in different ways. The documents are combined with some element of historical narrative — an introduction or a biographical essay, for example — that provides students with an analysis of the primary source material and important background information about the world in which it was produced.

Each book in the series focuses on a specific topic within a specific historical period. Each provides a basis for lively thought and discussion about several aspects of the topic and the historian's role. Each is short enough (and inexpensive enough) to be a reasonable one-week assignment in a college course. Whether as classroom or personal reading, each book in the series provides firsthand experience of the challenge — and fun — of discovering, recreating, and interpreting the past.

Lynn Hunt
David W. Blight
Bonnie G. Smith
Natalie Zemon Davis
Ernest R. May

Preface

This work presents students with an opportunity to examine the relationship between two key developments in European history. After 1517, Martin Luther's rebellion against the papal church shattered permanently the unity of a Latin Christian tradition that had endured for a thousand years, and the Reformation went on to recast the shape of Western Christianity in lasting ways. Second, in the mid-1520s, the German Peasants' War, the largest peasant insurrection in European history and the most massive popular rebellion prior to the French Revolution, shook the social and political foundations of central Europe. It expressed a profound desire on the part of subordinate groups in society for economic and social as well as religious transformation. Luther and other leading reformers opposed the commoners' attempt to advance their claims against the ruling elites by violence. Rebellion, to them, violated God's providence for political order and always harmed the innocent. But some reformers insisted that the secular authorities were as corrupt as the ecclesiastical and that the common people had the right to set aside oppressive conditions and defend themselves against the resulting assaults of "godless" rulers.

Society in early modern Europe, in which both the German Reformation and the Peasants' War took place, was a social formation pervaded by the influence of religion. Recent developments in the globalizing world of the twenty-first century have upset older sociological views that modernization leads inevitably to secularization or to a compartmentalization of life in which religion is separated from politics. Hence, the larger issues explored in this volume—the ways religious faith affects social issues and values, the use of religious principles and values to legitimate (or delegitimize) various forms of political action, the gap that can open between religious leaders and followers, and the ways in which popular movements take up and adapt new religious ideas—are all relevant to our own age. This study is designed to encourage students to think through these issues for themselves.

The book's Introduction provides students with a context in which to comprehend and evaluate the documents. Its narrative briefly surveys the condition of the German peasantry on the eve of the Reformation, with special attention to the peasants' precarious situation in a socioeconomic environment undergoing basic change as demographic pressure mounted, a commercializing economy posed new challenges, and the exactions of feudal lords and landlords increased. Luther's challenge to papal authority over the sale of indulgences generated immediate public support because of large-scale popular discontent with the political and economic power of the church in the Holy Roman Empire. The narrative follows the spread of the evangelical movement from its urban origins into the countryside, where rural commoners fused long-standing grievances with the new gospel message, culminating in the 1525 insurrection of the peasants, a brief but intense series of bloody pitched battles in which the lords quickly defeated the rebellious peasants. At the highpoint of the rebellion, Luther's condemning call for its immediate and merciless repression led to a spirited defense of the revolt's republican, even proto-democratic, foundations. Afterward, Luther defended his harsh stance against the reservations of his friends and followers.

The documents presented in Part Two include a variety of Luther's writings, as well as documents from other reformers, Roman clergy, and peasant bands. Each item is individually introduced by an explanatory headnote that helps students put the material in proper historical context. Selected in order to emphasize the linkages between religion and politics, the documents are arranged in chronological sequence to enable students to grasp the dynamic of a rapidly evolving social situation.

The volume also includes a map of central Europe at the time of the Reformation that emphasizes the political power of the church and a map of the areas encompassed by the Peasants' War that shows how the rebellion spread over time. The documents themselves include several illustrations, including the title pages of key tracts. Students are also supported in their understanding of the book's theme by a chronology of social and religious upheaval in the Holy Roman Empire from 1500 to 1526, a series of questions designed to stimulate reflection about the relation of the Reformation and the Peasants' War, and a select bibliography of works in English.

ACKNOWLEDGMENTS

Of the many people who contributed to this book, several merit special acknowledgment. My wife, Carol, patiently read the manuscript (more than once) and offered many detailed improvements. The criticisms and suggestions of several reviewers were critical to the development of this manuscript: Geoffrey Dipple, Augustana College; Lawrence G. Duggan, University of Delaware; Allan Galpern, University of Pittsburgh; Randolph C. Head, University of California, Riverside; and Ellis Knox, Boise State University. I am especially indebted to Geoffrey Dipple and Randolph C. Head, whose thoughtful critiques led me to rethink some important issues. My editors at Bedford/St. Martin's, Jane Knetzger and Heidi Hood, were unfailingly helpful, and a special word of thanks is due my developmental editor at Bedford/St. Martin's, Ann Kirby-Payne, who contributed to the book with encouragement, much editorial work, and good humor. Thanks also to Laura Kintz and Andrea Cava at Bedford/St. Martin's and to Nancy Benjamin of Books By Design for their assistance with manuscript preparation and production. Of course, I alone am responsible for any errors that remain.

Michael G. Baylor

Contents

Foreword   vii

Preface   ix

LIST OF MAPS AND ILLUSTRATIONS   xvi

PART ONE

Introduction: Germany's Dual Rebellions   1

Popular Discontent and the Need for Reform   3

The Reformation Break   8

The Gospel and Social Unrest   10

The Reformation in City and Countryside   11

The Onset and Spread of the Peasants' War, 1524–1526   15

The Aims of the Insurrection   20

The Peasants' Military and Political Organization   22

Luther, the Peasants' Defeat, and the Aftermath of the Rebellion   26

PART TWO

The Documents   33

1.   Unrest before the Reformation   35

   1. The Articles of the *Bundschuh* in the Bishopric
      of Speyer, 1502   35

   2. Title Page of Pamphilus Gegenbach's
      The Bundschuh, 1514   38

   3. The "Poor Conrad" Movement in Württemberg, 1514   40

2. The Reformation: Freedom, Authority, and Resistance 43

   4. Martin Luther, Ninety-Five Theses, October 31, 1517   43

   5. Pope Leo X, *Arise, O Lord* (Exsurge domini),
      June 1520   46

   6. Martin Luther, *To the Christian Nobility of the German
      Nation*, 1520   50

   7. *Greasing the Bundschuh*, 1522   55

   8. Martin Luther, *A Sincere Admonition to Guard against
      Rebellion*, 1522   57

   9. *Peasants Torturing an Indulgence Preacher*, 1525   59

  10. Huldrych Zwingli, *The Sixty-Seven Articles*, 1523   61

  11. Martin Luther, *The Rights of a Christian
      Congregation*, 1523   65

  12. Thomas Müntzer, *Sermon to the Princes*, 1524   68

3. Religion and Politics in the Peasants' War 74

  13. *Articles of the Peasants of Stühlingen*, Early 1525   74

  14. Sebastian Lotzer and Christoph Schappeler,
      The Twelve Articles of the Upper Swabian Peasants,
      March 1525   76

  15. Thomas Müntzer[?] and Balthasar Hubmaier,
      The Constitutional Draft, 1525   83

  16. Title Page of *The Memmingen Federal Ordinance*,
      March 7, 1525   85

  17. *The Memmingen Federal Ordinance*, March 7, 1525   87

  18. *The Document of Articles*, May 8, 1525   90

  19. *The Field Ordinances of the Franconian Peasantry*,
      April 24–27, 1525   93

  20. Thomas Müntzer, *Letter to the League at Allstedt*,
      April 26 or 27, 1525   98

  21. Michael Gaismair, *Territorial Constitution for the
      Tirol*, February or March 1526   100

4. The Debate on the Reformation and the Peasants' War **106**

22. Martin Luther, *Admonition to Peace: A Reply to the Twelve Articles*, April 1525   106

23. Title Page of *To the Assembly of the Common Peasantry*, May 1525   113

24. Christoph Schappeler[?], *To the Assembly of the Common Peasantry*, May 1525   115

25. Title Page of *Against the Murdering and Robbing Hordes of Peasants*, May 1525   128

26. Martin Luther, *Against the Murdering and Robbing Hordes of Peasants*, May 1525   130

27. Hermann Mühlpfort, Mayor of Zwickau, *Letter to Stephan Roth at Wittenberg*, June 4, 1525   135

28. Martin Luther, *An Open Letter on the Harsh Book against the Peasants*, June or July 1525   137

29. Albrecht Dürer, *Design for a Monument to the Victory over the Peasants*, 1525   140

APPENDIXES

A Chronology of the Early Reformation and the Peasants' War (1502–1526)   143

Questions for Consideration   146

Selected Bibliography   148

Index   **153**

Maps and Illustrations

MAPS

1. Central Europe in the Early Sixteenth Century   2

2. The German Peasants' War   18

ILLUSTRATIONS

Title Page of Pamphilus Gegenbach's *The Bundschuh*,
1514 (Document 2)   39

Greasing the Bundschuh, 1522 (Document 7)   56

Peasants Torturing an Indulgence Preacher, 1525 (Document 9)   60

Title Page of *The Memmingen Federal Ordinance*,
1525 (Document 16)   86

Title Page of *To the Assembly of the Common Peasantry*,
1525 (Document 23)   114

Title Page of *Against the Murdering and Robbing Hordes of
Peasants*, 1525 (Document 25)   129

Albrecht Dürer, *Design for a Monument to the Victory over the
Peasants* (Document 29)   142

PART ONE

Introduction:
Germany's Dual Rebellions

The German-speaking lands of the Holy Roman Empire were the scene of twin upheavals in the third decade of the sixteenth century (see Map 1). First, the Reformation shattered a Latin Christian religious and ecclesiastical tradition that had endured without lasting fissure for more than a thousand years.[1] An evangelical reform movement that began in 1517 with Martin Luther's posting of the Ninety-Five Theses, which contested the practice of selling indulgences or remissions of time spent in purgatory, rapidly escalated. After 1520 the break with Rome became final. The papacy declared Luther a heretic, and Luther spoke of the papacy as the "whore of Babylon" and the pope as "Antichrist." Luther, his followers, and those they influenced rejected the judicial and teaching authority of the Roman church, including its local episcopal representatives and their ecclesiastical courts, as well as central elements of its theology and practices.

Second, further political and social upheaval arose by the mid-1520s, in the wake of the onset of the Reformation. The German Peasants' War (1524–1526) was the greatest popular rebellion in European history prior to the French Revolution. At a time when a large national army (such as that of France) numbered in the tens of thousands, about three hundred thousand peasants and other commoners were enrolled in more than a dozen military bands at the height of the massive German insurrection in April, May, and June 1525. The number of people who supported and sympathized with the uprising, including many women who lent encouragement and logistical support, is impossible to

1

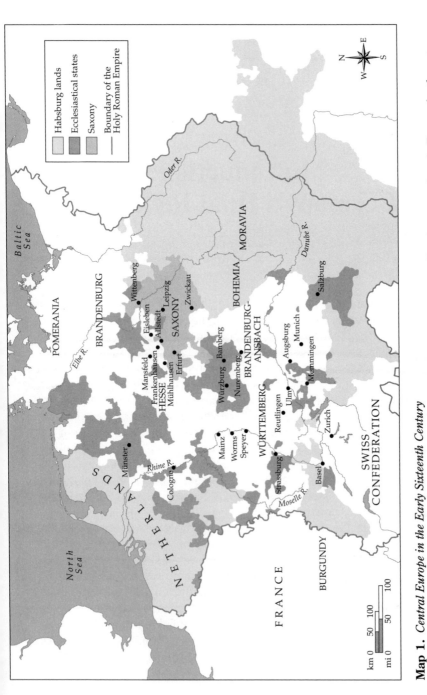

Map 1. *Central Europe in the Early Sixteenth Century*

In addition to the widespread holdings of the Habsburg dynasty, the Holy Roman Empire was unique in Europe for the extensive areas in which church prelates were also secular rulers.

estimate. For a time, it looked as though the entire political and social structure of the Holy Roman Empire—as well as its traditional religio-ecclesiastical system—might be overturned.

This study introduces students to the much-debated question of the relationship between these two momentous upheavals, one of which permanently altered the shape of Western Christianity, and the other of which was quickly crushed and apparently without major impact. From the sixteenth century down to the present, people have disagreed about the relationship of the sociopolitical upheaval to the Reformation. Luther's Roman Catholic opponents naturally accused the Reformation of bringing on the Peasants' War. Luther's heretical rejection of religious authority, they charged, inspired others to reject secular authority as well and opened the floodgates of general insurrection. Many prelates—archbishops, bishops, abbots, and so on—were simultaneously secular rulers. Monasteries as well as bishoprics were major landowners. So it was plausible to see the Peasants' War as the natural result of the Reformation.

Luther vigorously contested this view, sharply divorcing the rebellion from his cause of religious reform. He pointed out that from the outset he had cautioned his followers against resorting to violence and urged them to humbly accept rather than challenge the authority of secular government. As the revolt progressed, Luther concluded that it was the work of the devil. The peasants were dragging the gospel through the mud of their own selfish, carnal interests. He charged that bloodthirsty, fanatical preachers—agents of the devil—had seduced the lower classes into taking up arms, and that the devil hoped to use the Peasants' War to ruin the cause of the gospel, which Luther was reviving. Those who organized and led in the insurrection, on the other hand, argued that what they were attempting was to live according to the gospel. They insisted that God's Word prescribed how Christians should relate to each other in daily life, and that Luther himself had granted to local communities the right to decide for themselves the meaning of the Christian faith.

POPULAR DISCONTENT AND THE NEED FOR REFORM

Unlike many in the sixteenth century who assumed that divine or diabolical forces had brought about the mass rejection of traditional authority, contemporary historians no longer invoke supernatural forces to explain the Peasants' War, but they continue to debate the long-term causation of both it and the Reformation.

Both rebellions came during a major transition in German society. After about 1450, Germany's population and economy began to expand, and the expansion continued throughout the sixteenth century. This growth came after another long period (ca. 1300–1450) of demographic decline and economic contraction. The late medieval downturn, however, was also a time of market advantage for commoners. Peasants had easier access to more land on better terms, since land was plentiful due to the population decline and rents were low. The scarcity of labor also meant that real wages went up. For the lower classes, the long late-medieval slump resulted in greater personal freedom. To attract and keep labor, lords relaxed or eliminated the burdens of serfdom, the condition of legal semi-bondage that imposed special taxes and labor obligations on those who "belonged" to a lord. As lords leased out their lands rather than attempting to farm it themselves, they also relaxed their political hold on the settlements they ruled. The result was stronger communal institutions, as villages and towns assumed greater control over their own affairs.

Around the mid-fifteenth century, however, the socioeconomic tide turned, and the German economy entered the period of long-term expansion (ca. 1450–1630).[2] Population again increased, as did levels of production and exchange. Prices mounted, including land values and rents. The great inflation of this period, often termed a "price revolution," had several causes, including currency debasement and the production or importation of precious metals. But the most fundamental factor pushing up prices was the expanding population. The prices of foodstuffs and essentials ran well ahead of the prices of other products, especially manufactured goods. Real wages deteriorated, as price inflation outpaced wage increases, and the purchasing power of money fell.

General economic conditions, which previously had favored the peasants and the commoners, now turned against them. Landlords were not slow to take advantage of the shift. Both secular and ecclesiastical lords pushed up rents and entry fines (fees peasants paid on first taking possession of leased land, even if the land had long been in their families' possession). Lords also sought to reimpose serfdom's obligations and limitations on personal freedom and to reacquire land and usage rights that earlier had passed to peasant communities. Since lords and peasant communities were in competition for access to natural resources, tensions between them grew. Lords also attempted to control the churches in their domains by appropriating tithes and by ensuring that compliant clerics served as pastors.

As population increased, social tensions within villages also mounted. An economic gap grew between prosperous peasants with substantial holdings, on the one hand, and, on the other, cottagers (those who resided in the village but possessed little or no land) and day laborers whose family survival depended on working for the more prosperous. The geographic regions in which the Peasants' War occurred, especially at the outset, were mostly areas of partible inheritance, where a family's holdings were divided among heirs. This inheritance pattern could quickly lead to holdings that were no longer large enough to sustain the heirs' families, and the burden of rents, dues, and other obligations became especially acute.

The economic expansion brought other economic changes. A commercialized and more diversified agriculture developed. In addition to grain grown for sale in markets, some areas specialized in market gardening, wine production, and crops grown for textile manufacturing (e.g., flax, or woad and madder for dye). As commercialized agriculture expanded, the pressure of an expanding population and smaller family holdings also facilitated the penetration into the countryside of crafts and manufacturing, which formerly were mostly found in urban centers. As the German economy expanded from the late fifteenth century, large merchant capitalist firms also emerged and organized banking, long-distance commerce, cloth manufacturing, mining, and other enterprises along capitalist lines. Land was increasingly a component of the marketplace and subject to speculation. Capitalist entrepreneurs contributed to the economic expansion of the sixteenth century, but the commoners, miners in particular, seem to have experienced them mostly as usurers in lending, price-fixers in selling, rent boosters as landlords, and exploiters as employers. One strand that ran through both the Reformation and the Peasants' War was hostility to merchant-capitalists (see, e.g., Documents 6 and 20). Some peasants viewed cities in general as bastions of privilege, oppression, and exploitation.

Hence, for several decades prior to the Reformation and the Peasants' War, German commoners confronted deteriorating economic and social conditions, a period of adversity after one of prosperity. Commoners were more likely to be aware of this relative downturn in their condition and prospects than to be disturbed by their failure to participate fully in the more general economic expansion taking place.[3]

Political developments compounded the effects of economic change for commoners. The Holy Roman Empire—a multinational state formation in central Europe that many viewed as the continuation of Rome's late ancient Christian empire, with universal and sacral qualities—lacked a strong central government. Power lay mostly with the rulers of territorial principalities within the empire. It is doubtful that either the Reformation or the Peasants' War could have gained much popular traction without the empire's decentralized forms of rule. The one significant south Germany principality where little rebellion took place, and where the Reformation found little lasting support, was Bavaria, a large, comparatively centralized, and effectively organized principality. Conversely, where the Reformation succeeded, it had the support of sympathetic princes (e.g., Saxony) or urban elites, and where the Peasants' War was most intense, there was either an absence of strong princely government or government that the people perceived as arbitrary and tyrannical.

In the late fifteenth century, many princes began a new phase of state formation. They introduced a new legal uniformity in their principalities, overriding traditional local customs and oral culture. To pay for the growth of their administrative apparatuses, military establishments, and courts, princes also raised taxes. The territorial states possessed mixed or balanced constitutions in which territorial diets—representative assemblies of subject estates—checked the power of princes. Nevertheless, public taxation, private loans, and other revenue-enhancing devices the princes used imposed heavy burdens on subjects. The commoners' complaints could lead to rebellions against grasping princes (Document 3).

The Reformation gained its initial support especially in the empire's "free imperial cities," autonomous urban centers owing obedience to the emperor but not to a territorial prince. Many of these cities felt that the growing power of neighboring princes threatened their political autonomy and communal spirituality. Many free imperial cities were situated in the southwestern part of the empire, which was especially decentralized with a welter of small principalities and lordships. The Peasants' War had its origins and assumed its most radical forms in politically fragmented areas such as Upper Swabia and Franconia, where petty princes and landlords were one and the same. A count, abbot, or bishop was in a position to raise taxes, fines, and fees; to reduce commoners' rights of access to the basic resources of woodland, meadows, and flowing water; and to appropriate or sell off tithes and communal rights, reducing the authority of village government.

These long-term changes in the economy and politics may be the best explanation of the mood of malaise and discontent that hung over the cultural life of the empire in the late fifteenth and early sixteenth centuries. Many people shared a growing feeling that the times were out of joint and that a profound societal disturbance was impending. This mood was certainly heightened by a general awareness that a catastrophic external danger threatened the Christian society of the Holy

Roman Empire. Since the mid-fifteenth century and the fall of Constantinople (1453), the empire of the Ottoman Turks had extended its power north and west, up the basin of the Danube River. By the early sixteenth century Turkish power was threatening Hungary and then the Holy Roman Empire.[4] The psychological repercussions of this looming danger were profound—a sense that Christian society had lost its vitality, that the nobility had failed in its role as defender of the people, and above all that the clergy and the church had failed as mediators with the supernatural and had lost the favor of God. On a more mundane level, commoners were also embittered by the church's taxes and fees, perhaps especially when they were aware that these were leaving Germany for projects in Rome. The indulgence sale that Luther protested (Document 4)—a protest that large numbers supported—was designed to raise funds for the reconstruction of St. Peter's basilica in Rome.

A growing literature prophesying disaster and calling for reformation appeared. Much of it complained about the corruption of every estate in society and articulated a variety of reform projects. Luther's tract *To the Christian Nobility of the German Nation* (Document 6) incorporated some of the features of this literature. The reform projects usually included calls for a sweeping "reformation" that might return affairs to a largely imaginary golden age in the past, when all social estates cooperated harmoniously with one another in the fulfillment of their divinely ordained functions. The heavily moralistic literature bemoaned the rapacity of landlords and the arbitrary power of princes, the weakness and ineffective rule of emperors, the luxurious lifestyle and moral depravity of the clergy, the greed and chicanery of the merchants, the disobedience and turpitude of the peasants, and so on. This reform literature was characteristically backward looking and focused on the need to revitalize the moral character of the social estates and the institutional structure of the empire so that its medieval glories could be reclaimed. Despite some institutional and procedural changes in the governance of the Holy Roman Empire, the calls for political reform went largely unanswered. Emperors could enhance their authority only by curtailing the rights of the princes; princes refused to cede their growing power to a centralizing emperor.

From the last quarter of the fifteenth century, a series of local uprisings and popular disturbances called attention to a mounting crisis in society. In 1476, for example, the anticlerical prophecies of the shepherd boy and musician Hans Böhm at Niklashausen brought together pilgrims from the surrounding area of Franconia. The pilgrims directed their anger at the bishop of Würzburg, who responded by arresting and

executing the unfortunate youth. This episode was the first in a mounting series of localized revolts and conspiracies in the empire. Several
of these disturbances adopted as their name and sign the *Bundschuh*,
the bound (laced) shoe that was a symbol of the peasantry, and took
place in the Upper Rhine region in the empire's southwest (Documents
1 and 2). This region was close to Switzerland, where in the late Middle
Ages cities and rural cantons successfully established a federal repub-
lic through rebellion against their overlords, the Habsburg dynasty, a
lineage that ruled Austria and from which, since 1440, the emperors of
the empire had been chosen. German commoners were aware of the
Swiss success in freeing themselves from feudal rule and establishing a
canton-based, republican confederation of rural areas and cities.

Whatever these reform projects, complaints, conspiracies, and uprisings may tell us about the longer-term causes of the Reformation and
the Peasants' War, the earlier disturbances were on a very different
scale. What happened in the 1520s dwarfed them all. The difference
suggests that the more immediate context of controversy and public
agitation resulting from the start of the Reformation may have been as
important in the causation of the great popular upheaval as the under-
lying conflicts between the commoners and those who ruled them.

THE REFORMATION BREAK

Luther's disagreement with the traditions of the Roman church began
in the context of the monastery and the university. As a member of the
Augustinian order of friars that claimed to follow a rule written by St.
Augustine, Luther was profoundly influenced by the saint's theological
attack on the notion that people possessed a free will capable of decisions that contributed to their salvation. After he assumed a chair, provided by the Augustinians, in the theology faculty of the new university
of Wittenberg, Luther came to reject what he saw as the harmful influence of Aristotelian philosophy on Christian theology. Aristotle taught
that humans had the rational capacity to know and the freedom to will
virtuous actions. In his lectures and writings, Luther rejected this as
contrary to the teaching of the gospel. Lecturing on the letters of St. Paul
convinced Luther that it was a Christian's faith, not virtuous actions, that
led to salvation. The issue of indulgences—remissions of the temporal
punishment for sin, a punishment normally paid after death in purgatory—and especially the sale of indulgences, triggered Luther's conflict
with the papacy (Document 4). The conflict could have arisen over other

issues as well. As soon as Luther called the powers of the pope into question—and especially after he refused to retract his position unless he could be proven wrong on the basis of the scriptures—he was locked on a course that could only result in his condemnation (Document 5). Pope Leo X saw Luther as a stubborn heretic who, in addition to teaching erroneous doctrines about indulgences and other matters, was subverting both the teaching and the judicial authority of the church.

By 1521, when the papacy excommunicated him, Luther had worked out the essential principles of the new vision of Christian redemption that would define Protestantism.[5] At the center of his vision was the doctrine that the individual was saved *sola fide*, meaning "by faith alone"—that is, by relying for salvation only on the redemptive mission of Christ and not, as in traditional Roman Catholic teaching, on the combination of faith and meritorious works. In Luther's view of salvation, the Christian was entirely passive and dependent on God's freely granted gift of faith. This position cut the foundations from beneath many traditional religious practices and devotional activities. Having a saving faith in Christ and the grace that accompanied the experience of this faith were, for Luther, unmerited gifts from God, to which the believer was incapable of contributing.

Closely linked to this doctrine of salvation, by 1521 Luther had developed a form of Christian egalitarianism; that is, he concluded that all Christians were spiritually equal (Document 6). He attacked the clergy for exalting itself as a special order of society, superior to the laity, and for claiming special sacred attributes and a monopoly over the sacramental channels of divine grace. Luther's view—commonly referred to as the priesthood of all believers—destroyed the basis of the clergy's claim to special privileges and immunity from secular laws. When challenged about the authority on which he was disputing so many traditional beliefs and practices, Luther concluded that popes, even councils, can err. He rejected all human authority. The sole authority in matters of faith was, as he put it, the Word of God as found in the Bible and as understood by faith. This principle of *sola scriptura*, meaning "scripture alone," was another basic principle of Protestantism.

Luther's attack on traditional religion was radical, striking at the foundations of the medieval church as it had developed since the Gregorian epoch in the eleventh century. He rejected not only papal authority and canon law but also all forms of "works righteousness," the estate of the clergy, and the sacramental system. He and his followers contested many accepted practices and beliefs, not only the efficacy of indulgences but the entire doctrine of purgatory, not only the blessed character of relics and sacramentals but the holiness of any material object (excepting the words of the Bible), not only religious vows and pilgrimages but the whole enterprise of monasticism itself. In the early 1520s, neither Luther nor anyone else was sure how far the Reformation would go.

THE GOSPEL AND SOCIAL UNREST

The public controversy, which began with Luther's conflict with the pope, rapidly escalated. At the end of 1520, he and his followers at Wittenberg responded to the papacy's condemnation by burning volumes of canon law and scholastic theology. In 1521, the newly elected emperor of the Holy Roman Empire, the Habsburg ruler Charles V, called on Luther to appear before the assembled estates of the empire at the Diet of Worms. At this assembly, in a famous act of defiance, Luther refused to retract the controversial theological ideas he had expressed. The Diet, in turn, declared him an imperial outlaw and notorious heretic and passed a resolution forbidding innovations in religion. Following Luther's appearance at the Diet, his princely protector, Frederick the Wise of Saxony, staged a fake abduction and smuggled Luther away to the Wartburg castle, where he remained in seclusion for nearly a year, translating the Bible into the vernacular.

In the wake of Luther's excommunication, a remarkable wave of evangelical reform swept the Holy Roman Empire between 1521 and 1525. Powerful and localized revivalist movements outran the ability of Luther or anyone else to control or restrain them. They were generated by both clerical reformers and a growing group of lay participants, some of whom demanded sweeping extra-ecclesiastical changes. Luther influenced most of the reformers in one way or another, and they shared certain basic positions with him. All rejected papal power and the entire traditional structure of ecclesiastical authority. All were to some degree anticlerical and rejected a whole panoply of traditional practices. All called for the preaching of the "pure Word" of God without human addition. And all insisted that salvation was to be found in the experience of this pure Word, which was revealed in scripture. Many went further than Luther and formulated more far-reaching reform programs.

The reformers' audience did not play a passive, receptive role in this process. Frequently people demanded changes that they felt would enable them to lead more Christian lives. The central question that all had to deal with was what it meant to live according to the Word of God.

In an age in which all forms of authority rested on religious foundations and in which the categories of "spiritual" and "secular" had very different meanings than they do today, the Reformation message could not be divorced from social and political life. Many people insisted that the Word of God was relevant to the whole of life and that many areas of life in society needed fundamental reform. At this point, the message of the Reformation resonated with the anxieties and aspirations of the late Middle Ages. Luther's message turned into what historian Heiko Oberman called a "gospel of social unrest."[6]

A number of themes marked the emergent Reformation in Germany. One was violent anticlericalism and iconoclasm—the deliberate destruction of religious icons and images. Townspeople and students in the town of Wittenberg and elsewhere expressed their dislike of the non-reforming clergy by pelting them with stones and mud. They also interrupted sermons and the liturgy to challenge the authority of the clergy and express their dissatisfaction with the rituals of the old faith. Not only did people disrupt sermons and shout down priests; but they also subjected images, relics, and other religious objects to the same disrespect. They threw rocks through stained glass windows, tipped over holy water founts, subjected relics and holy images to ridicule and abuse, and then damaged or destroyed them.

The counterpart of this intense anticlericalism was that people came to see the laity, especially the simple, pious layman, as the best kind of Christian. Some reformers held up the uneducated commoner as superior to the learned, pretentious cleric. The "common man" became the new model of evangelical piety. The commoner worked with his hands, was simple and modest in his lifestyle, and was straightforward and upright in his manner, unlike the lazy clergy, especially the monastic clergy, who were parasites on society, lived a life of luxury, and perpetrated religious fraud against the laity.

THE REFORMATION IN CITY AND COUNTRYSIDE

In the beginning, the powerful evangelical reform movement was largely an urban phenomenon. Well-educated urban clergy led the drive for change. Towns were centers of the new technology of printing and the places where a literate laity was concentrated. In the early years of the Reformation, the number of tracts, pamphlets, broadsheets, woodcuts, and other printed materials produced by urban print shops skyrocketed. However, only a tiny fraction of the total German population (perhaps 5 percent) was literate, even in the vernacular.[7] Hence, even in urban settlements the message of the Reformation was mostly conveyed orally in sermons, public readings, debates, conversations, and arguments in marketplaces, taverns, guild halls, and other places where people gathered. Those without the skills of literacy also had access, of course, to the many woodcuts, engravings, and other visual means that conveyed the Reformation message.

At the outset, urban elites — mayors, town councilors, merchants, professionals, and other honorables — often supported the reform-minded clergy. But the evangelical movement also enjoyed the more broadly based backing of many artisans, craftsmen, and retail traders. These middling groups in the urban population provided the bulk of the urban support for the Reformation, as they were also the most numerous of any town's inhabitants.

The urban Reformation was strongly anticlerical, and one of its more remarkable features was the willingness of its clerical leadership to accept, sometimes to advocate, the abolition of clerical privileges and immunities. This, of course, was implied in Luther's rejection of the clergy as a separate estate in society (Document 6). The abolition of all clerical privilege produced legal equality and a level economic playing field. Hence, the preaching of the Reformation message, with its anticlericalism, contributed to the sense of egalitarianism and communal solidarity that was a basic component of urban reformation.

As the Reformation movement spread and diversified, and as a variety of reformers appeared in different venues with various visions of needed reform, differences and disagreements developed not only about the extent and the speed of change but also about who was authorized to institute it and what commoners might do if the existing authorities failed to make changes that they felt were required. Luther's own views about the relation of the Reformation to secular political authority shifted during the early tumultuous years of the Reformation. At the outset, in 1520, he had appealed to the lay ruling elite, the German nobility, as the proper social estate to direct the reform of a corrupted spiritual estate (Document 6). As early as 1523, Luther cautioned his followers against resorting to violence in the cause of the Reformation; they were not to take the law into their own hands (Document 8). Only the secular authorities had the right to institute changes. However, if secular authorities acted against the reforms he sought to bring about, Luther charged them with interfering in spiritual matters, where they had no competence; he counseled subjects to engage in passive resistance against such unjust laws.

In 1523, disappointed by the nobility's failure to support the Reformation cause, Luther expressed a set of radical ideals that appeared to reinforce and extend the communal and republican political forms that already existed in many towns and cities. He gave the local community or congregation two interrelated rights (Document 11): the power to determine the meaning of the Christian faith, which meant the capacity to define the changes that needed to be made in the name of the gospel, and the right to choose a pastor, who would preach the Word as the community understood it.

At the same time, in the Swiss city of Zurich, the reformer Huldrych Zwingli developed his own reform program, which included a version of this communal Reformation more radical than Luther's. Zwingli, like many others, insisted that needed reforms concerned not only personal salvation and ecclesiastical issues but the whole life of the Christian community as well. Zwingli's Sixty-Seven Articles, which he composed in 1523 for a public debate with Roman Catholic authorities, presented a distinctively urban-based and republican view of Reformation (Document 10). In Zwingli's view, the secular authority (in Zurich's case, an elected city council) was the proper agency to authorize religious changes. But he also stressed the right of the community to recall secular authorities who were failing to provide proper Christian leadership. This key principle was alien to Luther, who viewed politics through the lens of an individual who was subject to the authority of a hereditary prince, the elector of Saxony. Zwingli's Reformation principles, with their close connections between religion, urban society, and republican politics, had an immediate and widespread influence on other cities in the Swiss Confederation and the free imperial cities of the empire's southwest.

Zwingli envisioned citizens removing authorities who failed to provide good Christian leadership in ways sanctioned by a city's republican constitution. Not all reformers drew the line at this point. Among the major reformers, Thomas Müntzer—an early follower of Luther who became a penetrating critic—was perhaps the first to legitimize active resistance, in effect, armed rebellion against impious rulers. By the spring of 1523, Müntzer was pastor in the small market town of Allstedt. Here he instituted the first vernacular liturgy of the German Reformation. His sermons denounced the veneration of images and social injustice. At Allstedt, Müntzer formed a secret union or *Bund* that burned down a local shrine to the Virgin Mary. Catholic lords around Allstedt forbade their subjects from attending Müntzer's services and raided the homes and villages of those who did. In the summer of 1524 Müntzer seized an opportunity to preach to the princes of Saxony about their duty to defend good Christians from assaults by godless persecutors (Document 12). If they failed in this duty, Müntzer warned the princes, they would lose power. He later went on to argue that when their government failed them, people had the right to take "the sword"—the coercive power of secular government—and to wield it themselves. This was to legitimize a defensive but revolutionary seizure of power by the commoners.

It was especially through oral means that the peasants received the Reformation message as it moved from cities and towns into the countryside. This transition was absolutely necessary if the Reformation was to become a mass movement. Peasants constituted the vast majority of the population, probably at least 80 percent, and they lived mostly in small villages and hamlets with populations numbering from a few score to a few hundred. The German peasantry was overwhelmingly illiterate. However, although they were confined to an oral culture, they were not isolated from either urban life or written texts. Peasants came to towns for a variety of purposes, and there they came into contact with novel issues and ideas. They heard sermons advocating Reformation ideas, participated in discussions and debates, and examined visual propaganda for the Reformation. The peasants, in short, were readily capable of receiving the evangelical message, which they also interpreted according to their own needs.

In many parts of the empire, rural villagers had their own political association, the rural commune, which had acquired new strength and authority during the long agrarian depression of the late Middle Ages.[8] The village commune had considerable authority to manage its own affairs, including rights to administer justice. But there was tension in the village between those who had the right to participate in the commune's assembly—commonly male heads of households who were prosperous peasants—and those who did not. There was also tension between the village commune as a whole and the local lord, who limited the commune's authority and ultimately dominated it. The impact of Reformation principles in the countryside heightened both forms of social and political tension.

If cottagers and women were not members of the commune, they were of the village's congregation, to which the reformers gave religious authority. The Reformation's principle of the spiritual equality of all Christians made men and women, as well as cottagers, peasants, and lords, spiritual equals. In a society based upon religion, spiritual equality had social and political implications, and many people felt that

Reformation required the transformation of society as a whole according to the law of God. It is no wonder that many traditionalists charged Luther with inciting the commoners to insurrection (Document 7).

THE ONSET AND SPREAD OF THE PEASANTS' WAR, 1524–1526

The massive insurrection of the commoners began, some chroniclers later reported, at a specific time and place: in June 1524 at Stühlingen in the upper (or southern) region of the Black Forest, close to the Swiss border, on the estates of the count and countess of Lupfen (Document 13). In one version, the countess ordered the peasants to forgo agricultural work on their own plots and to spend a holiday gathering snail shells that she could use as spools to wind yarn. The peasants refused and began to organize themselves and voice their grievances.

To ascribe the start of the uprising to a single place, event, or seemingly petty grievance, however, obscures its genesis. Between spring and fall of 1524, a series of defiant and rebellious acts, both urban and rural, marked the onset of the storm. Sometimes the protesters justified these acts in terms of the new evangelical ideas, and sometimes they did not. In May 1524, the peasants at several locations in the Upper Rhine (the areas of the Black Forest, Hegau, and Klettgau) engaged in protest actions against payments and labor dues. For example, peasants subservient to the Black Forest abbey of St. Blasien refused to pay feudal dues and services. Their rejection of traditional ecclesiastical authority had immediate and direct secular implications, since the abbot was also the peasants' secular lord. There were also actions to the northeast, in Franconia, including Forchheim and the region around Nuremberg, in which peasants refused to pay tithes to the church or the lay appropriator of tithes. On one occasion, they burned tithes in the fields rather than hand them over. In September 1524, a rebellion occurred at the free imperial city of Mühlhausen in Thuringia when two evangelical preachers inspired an insurrection by discontented townsmen. The two were Heinrich Pfeiffer (or Schwertfeger), a native of the city and a former Franciscan monk, and Thomas Müntzer, who had recently arrived in Mühlhausen from Allstedt. Their party sought to overthrow the rule of the old city council and replace it with a new government of unlimited term of office that would administer the law according to the standards of divine justice.[9] In the summer of 1524, the Zurich city council also received reports that peasants in rural villages under the city's rule were refusing to pay their tithes and destroying ecclesiastical property.

In fact, the great rebellion lacked a single point of departure. As the ideals of the early Reformation were taken up in various places and fused with existing economic grievances and political complaints—or as these secular issues came to renewed expression in a context of intense religious debate and sweeping ecclesiastical challenge—disturbances of various kinds broke out. The causation of the great insurrection of the Peasants' War, then, is to be found in the convergence of old sociopolitical tensions with new Reformation ideals. In the Stühlingen uprising, which proved impossible to suppress easily, when the peasants drew up their grievance list, their sixty-two articles expressed mainly agrarian and secular concerns (Document 13). There was no directly identifiable Reformation influence. They complained about such matters as their loss of rights to woodland and commons, the denial of their fishing rights, and the field work and other labor obligations they were forced to perform. Elsewhere, the agitations had clearer links to the Reformation. Even the Stühlingen peasants denounced the institution of serfdom as a violation of Christian principles.

From the Stühlingen outbreak, the movement gathered continuous momentum, which may have led chroniclers later to see Stühlingen as the key triggering protest. The tenants of the region around Stühlingen assembled and chose Hans Müller from the village of Bulgenbach as their leader. Müller had military experience and was also a skillful organizer who realized that the peasants could best resist efforts to suppress their protest by gaining the support of others. Events had already begun to escalate, spinning outside the usual framework of negotiations between the rural commune and its lord. From August 1524, Müller began traveling the southern part of the Black Forest, seeking to extend the protest.

Among other places, Müller visited the small town of Waldshut, which was already in rebellion against its overlord, the Austrian Habsburgs. Waldshut was an early center of religious reform in the southwest, influenced by Zwingli and his coupling of demands for ecclesiastical change with those for a wider reform of society according to godly law as found in the gospel. Austrian authorities attempted to force Waldshut to give up its radical evangelical preacher, Balthasar Hubmaier, which it refused to do. Müller sought the support of Waldshut townsmen for the insurrection of the Black Forest peasants, and he succeeded in forming an alliance with the city. He also talked to the peasants in the Klettgau region, encouraging them to revolt, and traveled with his men across the Black

Forest to the upper Rhine. By October and November 1524, peasants all around the Lake of Constance were refusing feudal allegiances and dues. After these diverse beginnings in the latter half of 1524, the momentum of the insurrection temporarily diminished. The demands of the harvest and the impact of winter weather put a brake on events.

Early in 1525, the lords entered into negotiations with the insurgents at Stockach, but used these negotiations mostly as a delaying tactic. At the start of the uprising, the authorities were in a surprisingly weak position and they desperately needed time. The scale and intensity of the protests genuinely shocked the lords, and they pursued two strategies simultaneously. The nobles attempted to do what they could to raise sufficient troops to repress the uprising, but troops were difficult to come by on short notice; at the same time, seeing no realistic opportunity for immediate repression, they negotiated and made concessions to the rebels.

The inactivity of the colder months gave the insurgents time to reflect on their prospects, to listen to encouraging preachers, to formulate their demands, to seek alliances, and to plan. After he was expelled from Mühlhausen, for example, Thomas Müntzer traveled to the southwest via Nuremberg to preach to the peasants and provide them with political ideas. He stayed for several weeks in and around the small town of Griessen in the southern Black Forest, where he preached to the peasants of the Klettgau and Hegau regions. Perhaps he also made contact with Hubmaier in Waldshut, where the two may have drawn up articles on how the commoners could rule according to the gospel (Document 15).

Beginning in February 1525 and continuing through mid-July, the uprising renewed itself dramatically and violently. In February, the region of Upper Swabia went up in revolt, joining the peasants of the Black Forest and the area around the Lake of Constance, who returned to arms at this time. From March on, and from the southwestern corner of the empire near the Swiss border, the insurrection, like an avalanche, swiftly spread north and northeast, affecting Baden, Württemberg, the Palatinate, Alsace, Franconia, and Thuringia. It also spread eastward, jumping over Bavaria but producing revolts in the Alpine lands, especially the archbishopric of Salzburg and the Austrian duchy of Tirol (see Map 2). There was also an isolated eastern extension of the conflict in far-off Samland in East Prussia, in the kingdom of Poland.

It is now conventional to distinguish five main geographic theaters of the German Peasants' War: (1) the Upper Rhine (the Black Forest and Upper Swabia), (2) Württemberg and Franconia, (3) Thuringia, (4) Alsace and the Palatinate, and (5) the Alpine lands.[10] In each of these

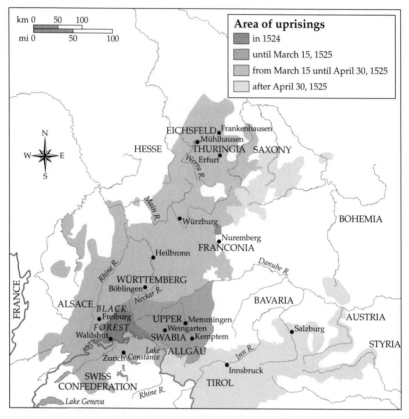

Map 2. *The German Peasants' War*

This map shows the extraordinarily rapid expansion of the peasants' insurrection in the first half of 1525. From its beginnings in the Black Forest, it quickly spread east into Upper Swabia and the Allgäu, then north into Alsace, Württemberg, Franconia, and Saxony and Thuringia, and then farther east into the Alpine lands of Tirol and the archbishopric of Salzburg.

areas the revolt had certain distinctive features and was influenced by the prevailing terrain and economy, as well as by the existing political and social structure. In some regions, the rebellion was more virulently anticlerical and in some less. In some areas it was more directed against serfdom and in some less; in some areas, the focus of grievances was the territorial principality as well as the local lords and in some not.

Despite these differences, which prevented the uprising from unifying into a single military force with one political goal, the rebellion was not a series of discrete regional risings that simply happened to coincide in time. Rebels in various areas communicated with one another, sharing ideas and demands. They used events elsewhere to inspire and encourage participation. They sought to communicate with their counterparts in other regions, developing, for example, document seals to assure the recipients of these communications that what they sent was secure and authentic. Occasionally they envisioned joint military strategies and political plans.

In its social composition, the German Peasants' War was one of the most sharply defined major rebellions of the early modern period. Far more than other late medieval and early modern revolts and revolutions—such as the Hussite rebellion in Bohemia (1420–1434) and the later Calvinist rebellions in the Low Countries (1568–1609), France (1562–1598), and England (1640–1660)—the German insurrection was a popular uprising, a revolt of subjects and commoners, *der gemeine Mann* (the "common man"), as the literature of the early Reformation put it. The revolt lacked the support of society's lords or governing elites. A handful of lesser nobles, some under duress, did join the bands of the peasants and sometimes acted as military leaders. But despite a few well-known individuals—for example, the knights Götz von Berlichingen and Florian Geyer—noble participation was so slight that it can be altogether discounted.

The case of the clergy is more complex. Ecclesiastical lords and prelates—archbishops, bishops, abbots, cathedral chapters, and so on—were among the chief targets of the insurrection, and a sharp anticlericalism suffused the entire uprising (Document 9). But if anticlerical violence permeated the revolt, a fair number of clerics also joined it, far more than the sprinkling of nobles who entered the ranks of the rebels. Most of the clerical sympathizers and participants came from the lesser clergy, especially those sympathetic to the principles of the new evangelical reform movement.[11] Clerics helped the rebels articulate their demands, often acting as secretaries to the insurgents and providing them with biblical legitimation for their programs and actions (Document 14). In some cases, they acted as political advisers, helping the insurgents plan strategy and goals (Document 20). Nearly always they sought to provide inspiration and consolation as military chaplains—to preach the Word, expounding the reasons for the rebellion and rightness of the cause, to inspire and to stiffen resolve before battle, to com-

fort the wounded and bless the dead. In Franconia, the peasant bands
included a whole contingent of armed clergy.

Despite this clerical participation, it was the lay commoners who gave
the insurrection its force and direction. It is too simple to describe the
participants in an undifferentiated way as peasants. The German *bauer*,
or peasant class, included all rural commoners: prosperous peasants,
who owned or leased a great deal of land; poorer cottagers and laborers, who held little; and a spectrum of intermediate groups. Peasants
included both those who were personally free individuals and serfs, and
some serfs were better off economically than some peasants who were
free. Many miners also joined the rebellion, especially those in regions,
such as the Tirol or parts of Saxony and Thuringia, where mining was
an important feature of the economy (Documents 20 and 21). Miners
were dissatisfied with their treatment at the hands of firms of merchant-
capitalists whose contracts with territorial princes permitted them to
exploit the mineral rights that the princes claimed over their territories.

In addition to miners, many townspeople, especially artisans, retail
traders, and urban day laborers, joined the rebellion. Many issues separated the urban participants and the rural; frequently, their economic
interests conflicted, and townspeople often scorned the personal depen-
dence that characterized rural areas where serfdom prevailed. But, as
the rebellion spread, the cases of Waldshut, Heilbronn, Memmingen,
Mühlhausen, and others showed the possibility of mutual support, and
some cities became centers of the rebellion.

THE AIMS OF THE INSURRECTION

At first, the insurgents were moderate in their actions. Down to March
1525, the revolt largely took the form of large peasant demonstrations—rallies at which those assembled voiced their grievances and
formulated their demands. Protest marches around the locality followed the demonstrations. The insurgents undertook these marches
partly in an effort to expand support for their cause. In the violence
that sometimes occurred during the demonstrations and marches, the
rebels mostly lashed out against property rather than people. Monasteries, churches, and noble castles were sometimes assaulted. Wine cellars were a favorite target of opportunity. Other actions destroyed icons,
libraries, and the written records of obligations and dues.

What did the rebels want? They composed or had others compile various lists of grievances and demands. Initially, the insurgents compiled

these demands as the basis for negotiations with their lords. One early program became especially widespread and influential. This was *The Twelve Articles of the Upper Swabian Peasants* (Document 14), which, as Peter Blickle argues, was the single most important political program of the Peasants' War and its major manifesto.[12] It was printed and then reprinted at least twenty-five times during the insurrection and was influential to varying degrees in nearly every region of the uprising, providing the nucleus of other programs. *The Twelve Articles* brought together the commoners' secular grievances and religious concerns. In this sense, it provides a key test for the relationship of the German Reformation and the Peasants' War. The early articles, especially, show the direct influence of the Reformation, and even in the later articles, reflecting long-standing grievances, the authors provided passages from scripture to legitimize their demands. The final article showed the influence of the Reformation in another way. It avowed that the peasants were willing to withdraw any article that could be shown to be contrary to the Word of God, and it raised the possibility of adding new demands that scripture might justify.

The program of *The Twelve Articles* was built around the overarching assumption that Christians had the right to live according to the gospel and its godly law. Earlier Bundschuh risings had sometimes advanced the principle that divine law or the law of God should be the template for social life. Now, infused with the evangelical zeal of the Reformation, the demand for godly law assumed a central place as the insurrection reached its most intense phase. The notion of God's law as a general legal principle, valid for all, unified the uprisings in several ways. First, godly law enabled the revolt to transcend merely local concerns and customary law. It allowed the subjects of different regions and diverse lordships, secular and ecclesiastical, to come together. It also provided a common framework for peasants and disaffected townspeople to join one another and suggested a vehicle for resolving their differences. Above all, of course, the demand that life be lived according to God's law mobilized vast sections of society not usually involved in politics, those whom the political elites felt had no right to express themselves concerning questions of rule. Conversely, godly law, as the commoners understood it, allowed them to group together their enemies. "The godless," as Michael Gaismair, the leader of the uprising in the Tirol, put it, were those who "persecute the eternal Word of God, burden the poor commoner, and impede the common good" (Document 21).

The program of *The Twelve Articles* was in some ways quite moderate and perhaps expressed especially the standpoint of prosperous peasant leaders who sought, through protest and demonstration, to bargain with their lords. It insisted that the peasants were not the source of the insurrection and that the "new gospel"—that is, the principles of the Reformation—did not lead to violence. The articles expressed a willingness to negotiate with lords concerning many grievances and to accept a lord's claims if he could properly document them. *The Twelve Articles* are also notable for what they leave out. Nowhere in the program did the peasants raise political demands in the sense of calling for an end to traditional lordship or for a wholesale recasting of the political order. On the other hand, as Peter Blickle has pointed out, there is also no doubt that, if realized, *The Twelve Articles* program would have entailed a revolutionary transformation of sociopolitical life.[13] It would have restructured landlord-tenant relations, eliminated all the disabilities of serfdom, and radically shifted the balance of political power and ecclesiastical control away from the lords and prelates in favor of the local community.

THE PEASANTS' MILITARY AND POLITICAL ORGANIZATION

The stereotype of a peasant rebellion commonly calls up an image of unruly mobs of uneducated and leaderless rural types rampaging around in a mindless and destructive frenzy, without aim, strategy, or organization. But the military and political organizations that the insurgents created to defend their cause and further their aims were innovative and well-considered. As the rebellion progressed, some among the leadership even envisioned a more far-reaching transformation of the political order than *The Twelve Articles* sanctioned.

The rebellion in any given region commonly began with a local assembly, consisting of either a formal convening of the village commune or a gathering of the subjects of a particular lordship. The rally was a larger and more spontaneous coming together of protesters that crossed the boundaries of individual villages and lordships. The suddenness, scale, and potential of this new development struck contemporaries, who remarked on it.[14] The rally then took on a defined organizational form through its formal constitution as a *Haufen*, or "band." Since the band crossed local political and legal boundaries, it expressed an inchoate regional identity, and bands usually defined themselves in terms of geographical regions—for example, the Black Forest, Hegau, Klettgau, Lake of Constance, Odenwald/Neckar Valley, and Tauber Valley bands.

What made the band unique was its combination of military and political functions in a single organization of subjects from several lordships.

In order to protect its participants and advance its demands, the Haufen organized itself, first of all, as a military formation. The band chose an officer corps, usually by election, to lead it. The leadership was modeled on the officer corps of the *Landsknecht* or lansquenet (foot soldier) formations of the time: mercenary infantry units in which the captains who exercised command were veterans chosen by the unit's members. Bands usually chose captains for their military experience, and some skilled military leaders emerged during the insurrection. However, there was often a lack of determination among commanders, evident at the battles of Weingarten, Königshofen, Saverne, and elsewhere.[15] In addition to captains, the bands created various other officers, many of whom they also elected, and drew up field ordinances or codes of conduct (Document 19). These other figures included paymasters, victualers and foragers, baggage masters in charge of supply lines and baggage trains, provost marshals in charge of discipline and courts-martial, masters of the spoils, and so on. The master gunner, in charge of artillery, was a key officer in set battles and siege operations. Wagon masters had responsibility for forming war wagons into a "laager" or circle, the best defense for an army caught in the open. Every band also included a number of preachers to sustain morale and often to act as secretaries. In one case, a contingent sought out a pastor, Johann Herolt, well-known for being sympathetic to commoners, and forced him to act as their preacher.

Peasant bands varied in size from four thousand to twenty thousand members, subdivided into companies under a captain or commander, then into troops or platoons under a sergeant. The band's smallest organizational unit was the troop or platoon, often based on the militia unit that village communes maintained. A troop could be as small as ten to fifteen men sent by a single village. Companies were often contingents sent by towns or groups of villages and could range in size from twenty or thirty men to five hundred or more. In some areas, bands instituted a rotation system, whereby a certain number of peasants from a given village served the Haufen at any one time, while others returned home to work. Contingents often rotated on a two- to four-week basis. This rotation system was practically essential for long-term campaigns, but it deprived armies of a chance to build experience and discipline.

The bands obviously faced the problem of how to feed and supply themselves. Whenever possible, they drew on the stores of their clerical and noble enemies. The insurgents raided and plundered numerous monasteries and castles, which they commonly destroyed. The plundering of monasteries often included much iconoclasm and the destruction of monastic archives and libraries, which commoners knew contained the written evidence of their dues and obligations. The bands were overwhelmingly male, but women also played important support roles. They cooked for the troops, helped outfit them, tended the wounded, and, as was not uncommon with Landsknecht armies, accompanied the bands as prostitutes. The bands' field ordinances included disciplinary codes that regulated their behavior on military campaigns (Document 19).

The Haufen was a dual-purpose institution; in addition to its military function, it had a political identity (Documents 17 and 18). The band was established as a political union or Bund by its members, who swore an oath; sometimes also passed beneath a banner, flag, or other symbol; and thereby obligated themselves to abide by the union's cause. The old symbol of peasant resistance and conspiracy, the peasants' bound shoe (Bundschuh), symbolized not only their social estate as peasants but also their union in a form that bound them to one another. In addition, the Bund had a religious dimension as a covenant between God and the membership, as well as an oath-based league, alliance, or federation of its members. Lords and rulers naturally saw the oath of Bund membership as an act of treason, a violation of the oaths of obedience they had their subjects swear to their own authority. To the lords, the covenant or union of commoners was doubly threatening. It crossed and invalidated the boundaries of existing law and political administration, and it was based on the notion of a nonhierarchical association of equals. In the latter sense, the peasants' unions mirrored the political principles of the Swiss Confederation, the *Eidgenossenschaft*, literally the "comradery of the oath." The peasants thus created their own polity, an extension of the original republicanism of the rural or urban commune, by swearing to adhere together and to regard one another as equals and as brothers (Document 15).

The principle that the members of the Bund were Christian equals was expressed in the form of the band's meetings. All members came together in a circle or ring, where no one had pride of place. As an egalitarian group, the members discussed matters of common concern, with the speaker entering the ring to have his say (as far as we know, Bund membership was limited to males). Bund membership afforded cottagers and smaller landholders positions of equality with the better-off, which may have been a source of radicalization during the rebellion (Document 18). At the conclusion of discussion and debate within the ring, a vote by all Bund members determined the decision to be taken. As a political entity, then, the Haufen incorporated political principles that expressed a republican, even democratic, impulse, although its democratic component should not be confused with nineteenth-century notions of individualism and the secret ballot, or twentieth-century ideas of gender equality.

The Bund formation possessed another feature of note. It was possible to extend it by uniting two or more bands with each other, forming a larger trans-regional union. This is what happened, for example, at Memmingen in early March 1525, when the bands from Baltringen, the Lake of Constance, and Allgäu came together to create a new Christian Union (Documents 15, 16, and 17). The formation of this new union illustrates how the insurrection possessed the capacity to create or reform political life beyond that of the geographically limited Haufen. The three regional bands united to form the government of a *Landschaft* ("territory"). The term *Landschaft*, when used in the politics of the early sixteenth century, was ambiguous. In regions where princes had already organized a territorial state, the Landschaft referred to the territorial diet, the state's representative assembly. Territorial diets usually included representation from three or four estates (clergy, nobles, townspeople, and occasionally the peasantry, as was the case, for example, in Baden and the Tirol). In regions of fragmented lordship, where there was no unified territorial state or diet, the Landschaft commonly referred to the inhabitants of a territory or region, either to the residents of the countryside (nontownspeople) or to the commoners in their entirety (all lay non-nobles).

This difference in the political environment of the areas engulfed by the revolt resulted in two different approaches to political reform.[16] When insurgent bands identified themselves as a Landschaft in regions where there were territorial principalities (e.g., Württemberg, Baden, Salzburg, or the Tirol), they were laying claim to the representation embodied by the existing territorial diet. That is, they either claimed the right to replace the old representative assembly, demanded to be included in such a diet, or asserted that the existing diet had greater power in the territorial state, restricting the power of the prince. Since they also claimed the right to ensure that rulers acted according to godly law, the insurgents were claiming, in effect, supreme or sovereign authority in the territorial state (Document 21).

A different and more innovative political transformation resulted in regions of fragmented lordship, where a unified territorial state was absent (e.g., in Upper Swabia, Franconia, or Alsace). In these locations, a Bund's claim to constitute a Landschaft had a different meaning. Here the peasant union designated itself as the government of the region from which its members came, in effect constituting itself as a newly formed territorial government (Documents 17 and 18). The political model for this development was the Swiss Confederation, in which local communities, rural and urban, came together in a corporative, sworn association of equals in order to attain common objectives, such as defense, while retaining their local autonomy and sovereign rights.

The territorial Landschaft, in either of these two senses, marked the outer limit of the political horizon of the insurgents. There were several attempts during the uprising for various Haufen to come together in larger, territorially conceived units. Similar to the peasants' "parliament" at Memmingen, there were actual or proposed meetings of representatives of different Haufen at Heilbronn and Würzburg. In Thuringia, delegates and messengers sought to coordinate the actions of different Haufen and to unite them politically. Of course, in regions where unified territorial states already existed, the political horizon of the rebels was generally limited to that state. There was, then, an ingrained localism in the politics of the Peasants' War, which contributed to the insurrection's failure.[17]

LUTHER, THE PEASANTS' DEFEAT, AND THE AFTERMATH OF THE REBELLION

Luther's initial response to the uprising was even-handed in its condemnation of both sides in the conflict (Document 22). His *Admonition to Peace*, written as a reply to *The Twelve Articles* (Document 14), blamed the princes and lords, especially the clerical lords, for causing the upheaval. Their greed and exploitation had pushed the commoners too far. But Luther also said the peasants were wrong to resist a political order created by God. He urged that the affair be resolved peacefully through mutual concessions.

The most important rejoinder from the insurgents' side to Luther's theory of politics and of the relationship of religion to social unrest came early in May 1525. This was the treatise *To the Assembly of the Common Peasantry* (Documents 23 and 24). The tract, which Christoph Schappeler may have authored, was the most important theoretical statement defending the rebellion.[18] It both argued for the legitimacy of rebellion and set forth a general constitutional theory for the political transformation the insurgents were seeking.

The conflicting views of Luther and Schappeler about the relation of religion and rebellion contain the heart of arguments that persist today. Luther insisted that violent uprisings are never justified. They always amount to what we would now call terrorism in that they inflict suffering and death on the innocent and threaten to produce a world of unlimited violence and chaos. Schappeler, by contrast, argued that people have a right of revolution — a right to set aside oppressive, unjust rulers, to create new governments, and to defend themselves when the displaced rulers use violence in an attempt to retain or recover their power.

When the rebellion broke out, the princes and nobles were ill-prepared for it. Their first attempts to recruit soldiers and mobilize for battle gained little traction. Hence, early on they were often willing to negotiate, even to make concessions. During the spring of 1525, however, the position of the lords improved. The imperial army of Charles V won a major victory against the French in Italy at the Battle of Pavia (February 24, 1525). This success allowed Charles to release the formidable army of the Swabian League from his Italian service so that it could return to Germany to deal with the rebellion. The commander of the Swabian League's army, Georg of Waldburg, was a skilled and strategically astute veteran. When his force came up against an alliance of the peasant bands near the Lake of Constance, he found himself outnumbered and on poor terrain for cavalry warfare. He successfully negotiated the Treaty of Weingarten (April 17, 1525) with the peasants. The rebels agreed to disband their Christian union and to pay their traditional dues until a negotiated settlement of their grievances could be reached. For Waldburg, this agreement was only a tactical concession. Having made peace with the major peasant force of Upper Swabia, the Swabian League's army then embarked on a series of campaigns against other peasant armies in the southwest. At battles fought near Böblingen (May 12) in Württemberg and in Franconia, the army of the Swabian League annihilated several peasant bands. The army then returned to Upper Swabia to settle scores with the peasants with whom it had earlier made a treaty.

Meanwhile, by early May, other princes had mobilized their armies and were coordinating their operations on a regional level. In Thuringia, the armies of Philip the landgrave of Hesse, the dukes of Saxony, and the counts of Mansfeld moved against the Mühlhausen-Frankenhausen band and inflicted a decisive defeat on it at the Battle of Frankenhausen (May 15), after which Thomas Müntzer was captured, tortured, and executed. At about the same time, Anthony, the duke of Lorraine, crushed the rebellious peasants of Alsace at the Battle of Saverne (May 17). By the end of July, the uprising was able to sustain itself only in the Alpine regions of the Tirol and Salzburg, where the mountainous landscape reduced the advantages that the princes' cavalry squadrons enjoyed on level ground. Here, the rebellion lasted into the summer of 1526.

For the most part, the major battles of the Peasants' War resulted in one-sided slaughters of the insurgents. At Frankenhausen, for example, the princes' artillery fire on the peasants' wagon laager caused the peasants to panic, break ranks, and flee toward the city. The lords' cavalry then moved in and mowed them down. Estimates suggest that about three thousand peasants lost their lives at Frankenhausen, as against only a handful for the army of the princes. Not all the pitched battles of the rebellion ended so decisively in princely victories, and occasionally—for example, at Herrenberg in Württemberg and at Schladming in Styria—the peasants came out on top. But such rebel victories were the rare exception.

The military failure of the rebellion resulted from several factors. The commoners frequently outnumbered the forces of the princes and were no less supplied with arms, which often included cannons and guns as well as edged weapons. They were, however, woefully deficient in cavalry squadrons, which commonly remained decisive in battle, despite the coming of cannons, pikes, and crossbows in the fourteenth century. Moreover, the peasant bands often lacked discipline and effective leadership. They were up against trained forces organized and commanded by those who were, by profession, the society's military leaders. The presence in peasant armies of experienced infantrymen, able to train the others and provide rudimentary leadership, was inadequate to overcome the difference.

In addition, despite incipient efforts to overcome the regional diversity of the uprising, peasant bands remained separated from one another, unable to provide mutual support and strategic coordination. The regions of the uprising remained separate theaters, functioning on different trajectories. As the rebellion was flaring up in one area, it was dying down in another. This gave the princes' armies the opportunity to deal with each band or grouping of bands separately. A massive bloodletting for the peasants resulted.

The outcome was not a foregone conclusion. During the insurrection, amid the fog of battle, the future was in doubt. In his *Against the Murdering and Robbing Hordes of Peasants*, Luther cautioned the princes to proceed swiftly and violently, but also with caution, fear, and prayers (Document 26). He urged the princes to kill as many insurgents as possible—it was, he said, just like killing a mad dog—yet he also wrote that no one could know for sure whether God was using the devil and the peasants to bring about the destruction of German society at the end of the world.

Although the nobles swiftly put down the rebellion with a horrific shedding of blood—observers estimated that a hundred thousand peasants died in the conflict—the aftermath was not entirely to the peasants' disadvantage. Leaders were executed, and many participants were maimed or fined. But it is not clear that the outcome had harmful long-term economic or social consequences, and the political and legal impact of the uprising is also difficult to reduce to a simple formula. Lords imposed new taxes and burdens only in individual cases. In some other cases, peasant demands were partly acceded to (Allgäu and the Tirol), and in others the peasants and their heirs enjoyed the benefit of obligations that came to be fixed in written contracts.

The Peasants' War did not force Luther to choose between the commoners and the political elites of Germany. Luther's profound fear of political disorder meant that where he stood was never in question. With the suppression of the revolt, some accused Luther of losing the support of the people, and even some of his friends and sympathizers charged that he had written far too harshly against the peasants (Document 27). Luther's rejoinder conceded nothing: those who showed any sympathy with the rebels were "fellow-travelers" inspired by the devil (Document 28). Luther's support of the princes' repressive violence in 1525 also did much to determine the future direction of the German Reformation and the structure of the Lutheran church in Germany. Down to 1525 no German prince explicitly supported Luther's call for religious and ecclesiastical change, not even Frederick the Wise. From 1525 on, some princes gave Luther their support and introduced the reforms he sought, but under their political control.

As the princes came aboard the Reformation, Luther also altered his views on the proper function of princes in ecclesiastical affairs. In 1523, as Luther formulated his doctrine of the two kingdoms, he insisted that secular rulers had no authority to interfere in spiritual affairs. By 1526, just after the insurrection, he reverted to the position he held in 1520 (Document 6) and announced that princes could act as "emergency bishops" to bring about needed Reformation in their principalities. The result was that the church princes ruled over became, in effect, a branch of the state. The defeat of the commoners in the Peasants' War, in short, began a protracted period of more conservative, orderly, and hierarchically directed Reformation.

State supervision of ecclesiastical life in the aftermath of the Peasants' War also meant deploying the power of the state to go after religious dissidents and deviants. As many peasants and urban craftsmen abandoned their hopes of participating in and shaping public religious and political life, they fell into superficial conformity and religious apathy. However, a dissenting minority sought to continue the communal and popular ideals of the early Reformation and the Peasants' War. These dissenters commonly expressed their rejection of the established churches by disavowing the validity of infant baptism, the ritual by which authorities everywhere made sure that church and society coincided. The authorities fiercely persecuted these "Anabaptists" or "rebaptisers" as dangerous subversives and a threat to public order.[19] In their attitude toward the authorities, the persecuted sectarians oscillated between the adoption of nonviolent resistance, which became the norm for most of these powerless and persecuted minorities, and infrequent efforts to revivify the cause of the commoners through violence.[20] In the stigmatized communities of Anabaptist dissenters, part of the German commoners' effort to recast public life by infusing it with their understanding of the principles and values of the German Reformation survived. Germany's dual rebellion, however, had clearly come to a parting of the ways.

NOTES

[1] The Hussite movement in Bohemia in the early fifteenth century represented a major break in this tradition, one that Luther and the other sixteenth-century reformers quickly came to view in a positive light. But the *Compacta* of 1436, negotiated at the Council of Basel, reconciled the Hussites with Rome, which recognized them as true sons of the church and conceded to them the cup in Communion.

[2] An accessible survey of social and economic trends during this time is Bob Scribner, ed., *Germany: A New Social and Economic History*, vol. 1, *1450–1630* (London: Arnold, 1996).

[3] This account of the mentality of the rural commoner seems more accurate than the view that peasants were resentful because their enrichment proceeded less rapidly than that of others in the society at a time of economic growth and prosperity. For this view, see Eugene F. Rice Jr. and Anthony Grafton, *The Foundations of Early Modern Europe, 1460–1559*, 2nd ed. (New York: W. W. Norton, 1994), 73–75.

[4] By the end of the 1520s a Turkish army had overrun Hungary and laid siege to Vienna.

[5] The term *Protestant* was not coined until the end of the 1520s. In 1529, a majority of the estates of the empire, assembled at a diet in the city of Speyer, condemned the followers of Luther for introducing religious innovations. The princes and cities that supported Luther then issued a formal "protest" and declared they would follow the will of God; these estates came to be called the "protestant estates."

[6] Heiko Oberman, "The Gospel of Social Unrest," in Bob Scribner and Gerhard Benecke, eds., *The German Peasants War 1525—New Viewpoints* (London: George Allen and Unwin, 1979), 39–51.

[7] Ulinka Rublack estimates that 30 percent of urban males may have been literate, but that 90 percent of the German population lived in the countryside, where illiteracy

was the norm. Ulinka Rublack, *Reformation Europe* (Cambridge: Cambridge University Press, 2005), 45.

[8] On the development of the late medieval German rural commune, see especially Peter Blickle, *Obedient Germans? A Rebuttal. A New View of German History*, trans. Thomas A. Brady Jr. (Charlottesville: University Press of Virginia, 1997).

[9] This revolt quickly collapsed, in part because those engaged in it failed to include in their demands anything that might gain the support of Mühlhausen's peasantry, which came to the aid of the old ruling elite.

[10] Tom Scott and Bob Scribner, eds. and trans., *The German Peasants' War: A History in Documents* (Atlantic Highlands, N.J.: Humanities Press International, 1991), 19–53.

[11] For this important aspect of the insurrection, see especially Justus Maurer, *Prediger im Bauernkrieg* (Stuttgart: Calwer Verlag, 1979).

[12] Peter Blickle, *The Revolution of 1525: The German Peasants War from a New Perspective*, trans. Thomas A. Brady Jr. and H. C. Erik Midelfort (Baltimore: Johns Hopkins University Press, 1981), 18–22.

[13] Ibid., 133.

[14] Scott and Scribner, *The German Peasants' War*, 15. The German term for this rally was *Zusammenlaufen*, literally a "running together."

[15] Ibid., 59.

[16] Horst Buzello, *Der deutsche Bauernkrieg von 1525 als politische Bewegung mit besonderer Berücksichtigung der anonymen Flugschrift an die Versammlung gemayner Pawerschafft* (Berlin: Colloquium Verlag, 1969).

[17] The major exception to this localism occurred in the context of a peasant parliament planned for Heilbronn in early May 1525. In anticipation of this meeting, two *Haufen* secretaries who were former officials, Wendel Hippler and Friedrich Weygandt, drafted proposals for the social and political reform of the Holy Roman Empire as a whole. But as the military tide of the conflict shifted, the Heilbronn parliament proved abortive. In general, the peasants thought in terms of neither the Holy Roman Empire nor the universal church. Thomas A. Brady Jr., *German Histories in the Age of Reformations, 1400–1650* (Cambridge: Cambridge University Press, 2009), 191.

[18] The theoretical importance of the tract is discussed in Buzello, *Der deutsche Bauernkrieg von 1525 als politische Bewegung*, 92–125. Historians have debated the authorship of the tract. For some time, the controversy was whether Andreas Bodenstein von Karlstadt wrote the work. More recently and more convincingly, Peter Blickle has argued for the authorship of Christoph Schappeler, who also contributed to *The Twelve Articles*. Peter Blickle, "Republiktheorie aus revolutionärer Erfahrung (1525)," in Peter Blickle (Hrsg.), *Verborgene republikanische Traditionen in Oberschwaban* (Tübingen: Bibliotheca Academica Verlag, 1998), 195–210.

[19] Roman law gave civil authorities the right to inflict the death penalty on those guilty of rebaptism (i.e., "anabaptism"). Of course, in the view of the dissenters, infant baptism was meaningless and did not count as baptism. Only an adult's or believer's baptism was authentic.

[20] The most famous episode of violence was the Anabaptist revolution in the city of Münster in Westphalia in 1533–1534. Closer to the end of the Peasants' War, in 1527 authorities at Erfurt uncovered a plot to overthrow the government.

PART TWO

The Documents

1

Unrest before the Reformation

1

The Articles of the Bundschuh *in the Bishopric of Speyer*

1502

*From the late fifteenth century, peasant unrest, urban disturbances, and a
literature of grievance and reform provide evidence of increasing dissatisfaction with social conditions in the German-speaking lands of the Holy
Roman Empire. After the turn of the sixteenth century, the Upper Rhine
area in the southwestern part of the empire was the scene of a number
of* Bundschuh *conspiracies. The Bundschuh, the bound (laced) shoe of
the country folk, was a symbol of the social estate of the peasantry that
came to connote more than peasant life and its attendant hardships. It
also became synonymous with the peasants' desire for reform and with the
illegal political organizations they undertook to attain it. The chief Bundschuh conspirator of the early sixteenth century, Joss Fritz, a serf of the
bishop of Speyer, gained such a reputation as an inciter of social unrest
that some have questioned whether he was an actual person or a mythical
figure to whom authorities automatically ascribed rural unrest.*

*In 1502 Fritz organized a peasant rebellion in the bishopric of Speyer
to protest the bishop's exactions. His plan was to attack the city of Bruchsal and towns and castles in the principality of Baden. The slogan on
the rebels' flag summarized their fundamental aim: "Lord, stand by Thy
divine justice"; in other words, they wanted to do away with all human
laws and to be subject only to godly law, a demand that later resurfaced*

Gerald Strauss, ed. and trans., *Manifestations of Discontent in Germany on the Eve of the
Reformation* (Bloomington: Indiana University Press, 1971), 144–47.

in the Peasants' War. Before the peasants launched the attack on Bruchsal, the authorities learned of the plan and repressed the Bundschuh. Fritz managed to escape, but confessions extracted from more than a hundred members of the conspiracy are the basis of the following articles, which a hostile scribe recorded.

The first article of their confession: They said that the principal reason for their entering into this association of the *Bundschuh* was their desire to abolish every remaining yoke of servitude and, following the example of the Swiss, to gain their liberty through the use of arms, as soon as their number had grown sufficiently and they had gained confidence in their ability to win in combat.

2. They confessed that those who joined their organization must say five Paternosters with the Ave Maria,[1] kneeling, in memory of the five principal wounds of Jesus Christ, so that God might grant success to their endeavors.

3. They chose Our Lady, the Virgin Mary, and St. John as patron saints. In order to have a secret sign of recognition, they decided on the following password: One conspirator asks another, "What is your name?" The other, if he belongs to the conspiracy, replies, "The priests are to blame." Oh, the sinfulness of the peasant mind! What a bane it has always been to the clergy!

4. During and after torture they confessed that it was their intention to annihilate all authority and government. They had decided that, as soon as their number had grown large enough, their bands would fall upon anyone opposed to them and kill without mercy all those who dared resist.

5. They said that they had decided to attack first the city of Bruchsal in the bishopric of Speyer, where, they boasted, half the inhabitants were sympathetic to them. Having gained Bruchsal, they planned to proceed, armed, against the Margraviate of Baden and devastate everything that lay in their path.

6. They had resolved to pillage monastic and ecclesiastical possessions, also the properties of the clergy, and to divide the booty among themselves. They wished to humiliate the servants

---

[1] Latin terms for the common prayers, Our Father and Hail Mary.

of the Church and to reduce them in number by killing and driving out as many as possible.

7. They had agreed among themselves that, once enough peasants had assembled, they were not to stay in any one spot longer than twenty-four hours following a victorious battle but to move on from place to place until they had subjected the whole country to their conspiracy.

8. Such great confidence had they in their endeavor that they took it for certain that, once the war had broken out, no subjects would resist them; they believed, on the contrary, that peasants, burghers,[2] and townsmen would freely join their association out of the love of liberty which all men share.

9. They confessed that they had decided among themselves to come together at dawn on Friday, the day before St. George's day [April 22], to launch their assault on the city of Bruchsal. And they would have succeeded in their objective, due to the number of sympathizers among the citizens, had a chance occurrence not prevented the plot from being carried out.[3]

10. They confessed that their main targets were monasteries, cathedral churches, and the clergy in general. These they intended to strip of their properties and deprive of their authority. They also resolved never again to pay a tithe, either to the clergy or to secular lords and nobility.

11. They confessed that they had decided among themselves to take by force of arms all the freedoms they desired and would henceforth refuse to tolerate any man's dominion over them. They would no longer pay interest, remit tithes or taxes, nor pay tolls or dues of any kind. They wished to be completely quit of all duties and tributes.

12. They demanded that hunting, fishing, grazing, lumbering, and every other thing that had become a princely prerogative be returned to the public so that a peasant might hunt and fish

---

[2] Burghers were urban dwellers who possessed the rights and privileges of citizenship in the town where they resided.

[3] According to Gerald Strauss, a conspirator divulged the plans for the conquest of Bruchsal during confession. Notified by the priest, the authorities arrested the ringleaders and suppressed their followers with the common punishments for treason of death for men and exile for women and children. Gerald Strauss, ed. and trans., *Manifestations of Discontent in Germany on the Eve of the Reformation* (Bloomington: Indiana University Press, 1971), 146, n. 1.

whenever and wherever he had a mind to, without being hindered or oppressed by anyone.

13. The peasants agreed that their band would march first of all against the Margrave of Baden, the Bishop of Speyer, and the monks and clergy in the vicinity. Whoever undertook to resist them would be killed mercilessly as a disobedient and seditious enemy of divine justice.

2

Title Page of Pamphilus Gegenbach's The Bundschuh

1514

In 1514, the author Pamphilus Gegenbach published a pamphlet describing a Bundschuh *conspiracy against the city of Freiburg im Breisgau in the region of the Black Forest. The work's fulsome title was* The Bundschuh: This Booklet Tells of the Evil Undertaking of the Members of the Bundschuh, How It Began and Ended, and Its Consequences. *The illustration shows a peasant with a flag or banner featuring an image of the crucifixion at its center and imperial and papal coats of arms at the sides. On the ground on the left side of the title page is a depiction of the laced shoe (*Bundschuh*) of the peasantry. The plaque to the right of the figure gives the year.*

Der Bundtschu
Diß biechlein sagt von dem bö
sen fürnemen der Bundtschuher/wye es sich
angefengt geendet vnd aus kumen ist.

3

The "Poor Conrad" Movement in Württemberg
1514

---

*Like the conspiracies of Joss Fritz, the "Poor Conrad" (Arme Konrad)
movement in Württemberg was more than a purely peasant phenomenon.
"Conrad" (Konrad or Kunz) was a general name for the German commoner. The 1514 rebellion, which included townspeople as well as peasants,
was a product of misgovernment by Ulrich, the duke of Württemberg.
In 1514, the duke attempted to increase his revenues from excise taxes
by manipulating the duchy's weights and measures. For example, if the
official pound weighed fourteen ounces instead of sixteen, more pounds
of goods would be sold, and a tax levied per pound would thus yield more
revenue. This alteration enraged the duke's subjects. It came on the heels
of a series of oppressive actions by ducal officials, who violated local
customs in an effort to centralize government. The duke's subjects rose in
protest. The rebellion was cut short when the duke reached an agreement
with urban notables; called a meeting of the* Landtag, *the diet or assembly, of the duchy's estates; and arrested and executed many involved in the
rebellion. The following articles were among the popular grievances that
the estates presented to the duke at the diet.*

---

8. We ask that the councilors and secretaries of the chancellery
   [of the duchy of Württemberg] be chosen from among honest,
   pious, knowledgeable, and competent persons who must not be
   related to one another by blood or friendship (as has been the
   custom in the past and is still at present). They should be concerned only with advancing the honor of God and the common
   interest of our gracious sovereigns and their country rather
   than with seeking their own advantage, as they have been doing
   in the past by means of the imposition of new taxes and burdens
   profitable to themselves but painful to the country. . . .

Gerald Strauss, ed. and trans., *Manifestations of Discontent in Germany on the Eve of the
Reformation* (Bloomington: Indiana University Press, 1971), 151–53.

15. Due consideration should be given to the plague of learned lawyers that has been infesting legal business in every court in the land, the result being that the cost of litigation, which, twelve years ago, came to only a few pennies, runs nowadays to ten gulden[1] or more. These are grievous innovations for the common man, and they ought to be brought to an end; if not, each village will, before long, need to hire one or two doctors of law to handle its judicial business.

16. Inasmuch as these learned lawyers and jurists have caused disruption and disarray among the agreements and other ancient customs and usages in our towns and villages — much to the hurt and disadvantage of the common man — there should be instituted, drawn up, and promulgated a general reformation and renovation of the laws of our land. If not, towns and villages should be left to their wonted customs, laws and courts, as these have come down to us from ancient times, lawyers and doctors of jurisprudence notwithstanding.

17. We ask that our gracious prince and lord endow the posts of bailiff and tax collector with good salaries and appoint to these offices only honorable, God-fearing, competent, and affluent persons, who are well disposed toward the common man and will administer their offices honestly, performing all their duties in their own persons and not through deputies or vicars. . . .

28. Soldiers on horseback and huntsmen should be required to proceed along roads and pathways rather than cross-country through our fields and meadows, for in riding over our land they cause great damage to crops, fruits, and other products. The destructive practices of conducting the chase and hunt across our fields ought also to cease and be forbidden. . . .

40. Our gracious lord ought furthermore to make a law concerning wild game on our properties, especially for the summer months from Easter to autumn, when the poor man's fields and products are commonly destroyed by game and no remission is allowed him in the payment of rent and dues.

---

[1] The gulden was the official gold coin of the Holy Roman Empire, equivalent to the Dutch guilder. Its value fluctuated.

41. Item: No official in our gracious lord's chancellery accepts complaints concerning wild game or actions of the forester,[2] nor do they undertake to rectify any of the above-mentioned abuses. Instead they refer such complaints to the foresters themselves, who are therefore in a position to act as prosecutors, witnesses, and judges all at once, much to their own advantage and to the harm of the common man.

42. Inasmuch as foresters, their assistants, and other officials have been appropriating some common lands and brooks, although these have always been free and open to all, and have proceeded to award these to whomever they please, it is our humble plea that such brooks and common lands be made free again, as they were in ancient times. . . .

46. Recently the foresters have begun to sell the brushwood left on the ground after firewood has been collected. In former times the poor had always been entitled to gather the brushwood, a custom less injurious to our lord's forests than the new practice, for what the foresters now sell as brushwood is better stuff than firewood used to be. This practice damages the interests of our gracious lord and infringes the rights of the poor, whereas it is of great profit to the forester.

47. In many places the foresters employ assistants and retainers, though in the old days no such sub-officials were known in the territory. Moreover, many of these assistants are disorderly persons, inclined to exploit and punish the poor. It should also be remembered that our gracious princes are obliged to remunerate these assistants with good money, which is a considerable expense and a loss to their treasury. . . .

50. These foresters commit a further abuse in allowing pigs from other regions to be led to our acorn feeding places, much to the harm and disadvantage of the poor folk in our territory. We ask that this practice be halted and no outsiders' pigs be let into our forests.

---

[2] Foresters were officials responsible for the care and management of forests. They had the power to permit or deny access to forests and to set conditions and prices for the use of the key natural resource of the woodlands.

2

The Reformation: Freedom, Authority, and Resistance

4

MARTIN LUTHER

Ninety-Five Theses

October 31, 1517

---

*Historians conventionally mark the birth of the Protestant Reformation
with Martin Luther's posting of his Ninety-Five Theses against the sale of
indulgences (or* Disputation on the Power and Efficacy of Indulgences*)
on the eve of All-Saints Day in 1517. Some authorities question whether,
as legend has it, the theses were nailed to the door of the castle church in
Wittenberg. Others point out that even if Luther did post them this way, it
was hardly a dramatic and defiant act of protest; the castle door was the
university's bulletin board, and Luther could only have been announcing
to a university audience that he wished to propose for debate a variety
of theses that he composed in Latin on a fairly arcane topic. Surely the
theses did not represent anything like a systematic or clearly organized
manifesto for rebellion. Nevertheless, the Ninety-Five Theses did mark
the onset of a sustained and public protest against the powers of the pope
and the traditions of the Roman Catholic Church. The theses were quickly
translated into the vernacular and printed and reprinted across the
Holy Roman Empire and beyond. The humanist movement in northern
Europe and the lay readership it cultivated were especially prominent
in turning Luther's theses into a public affair and in making a theology*

Martin Luther, *Luther's Works*, ed. Jaroslav Pelikan and Helmut T. Lehmann, trans.
Charles M. Jacobs, rev. Harold J. Grimm (St. Louis: Concordia, 1955), 31:25–33.

professor at an obscure provincial university the center of a mounting controversy about the leadership of Europe's Christian society and, ultimately, about the basis of salvation.

Out of love and zeal for truth and the desire to bring it to light, the following theses will be publicly discussed at Wittenberg under the chairmanship of the reverend father Martin Luther, Master of Arts and Sacred Theology and regularly appointed Lecturer on these subjects at that place. He requests that those who cannot be present to debate orally with us will do so by letter.

In the Name of Our Lord Jesus Christ. Amen.

1. When our Lord and Master Jesus Christ said, "Repent" [Matt. 4:17], he willed the entire life of believers to be one of repentance.

2. This word cannot be understood as referring to the sacrament of penance, that is, confession and satisfaction, as administered by the clergy. . . .

5. The pope neither desires nor is able to remit any penalties except those imposed by his own authority or that of the canons.

6. The pope cannot remit any guilt, except by declaring and showing that it has been remitted by God; or, to be sure, by remitting guilt in cases reserved to his judgment. If his right to grant remission in these cases were disregarded, the guilt would certainly remain unforgiven. . . .

8. The penitential canons are imposed only on the living, and, according to the canons themselves, nothing should be imposed on the dying. . . .

18. Furthermore, it does not seem proved, either by reason or Scripture, that souls in purgatory are outside the state of merit, that is, unable to grow in love.

19. Nor does it seem proved that souls in purgatory, at least not all of them, are certain and assured of their own salvation, even if we ourselves may be entirely certain of it.

20. Therefore the pope, when he uses the words "plenary remission of all penalties," does not actually mean "all penalties," but only those imposed by himself.

21. Thus those indulgence preachers are in error who say that a man is absolved from every penalty and saved by papal indulgences. . . .

23. If remission of all penalties whatsoever could be granted to any-one at all, certainly it would be granted only to the most perfect, that is, to very few.

24. For this reason most people are necessarily deceived by that indiscriminate and high-sounding promise of release from penalty. . . .

27. They preach only human doctrines who say that as soon as the money clinks into the money chest, the soul flies out of purgatory.

28. It is certain that when money clinks in the money chest, greed and avarice can be increased; but when the church intercedes, the result is in the hands of God alone. . . .

32. Those who believe that they can be certain of their salvation because they have indulgence letters will be eternally damned, together with their teachers. . . .

36. Any truly repentant Christian has a right to full remission of penalty and guilt, even without indulgence letters.

37. Any true Christian, whether living or dead, participates in all the blessings of Christ and the church; and this is granted him by God, even without indulgence letters. . . .

43. Christians are to be taught that he who gives to the poor or lends to the needy does a better deed than he who buys indulgences. . . .

48. Christians are to be taught that the pope, in granting indul-gences, needs and thus desires their devout prayer more than their money.

49. Christians are to be taught that papal indulgences are useful only if they do not put their trust in them, but very harmful if they lose their fear of God because of them.

50. Christians are to be taught that if the pope knew the exactions of the indulgence preachers, he would rather that the basilica of St. Peter were burned to ashes than built up with the skin, flesh, and bones of his sheep.

51. Christians are to be taught that the pope would and should wish to give of his own money, even though he had to sell the basilica

of St. Peter, to many of those from whom certain hawkers of
indulgences cajole money.

52. It is vain to trust in salvation by indulgence letters, even though
the indulgence commissary, or even the pope, were to offer his
soul as security. . . .

66. The treasures of indulgences are nets with which one now
fishes for the wealth of men. . . .

94. Christians should be exhorted to be diligent in following Christ,
their head, through penalties, death, and hell;

95. And thus be confident of entering into heaven through many
tribulations rather than through the false security of peace
[Acts 14:22].

5

POPE LEO X

"Arise, O Lord" (Exsurge domini)

June 1520

*The Dominican order in Germany countered Luther's protest against the
sale of indulgences (Document 4) by citing the affair to Rome for a decision. The papacy initially attempted to negotiate for Luther's retraction
and silence, but these efforts dissolved as public controversy mounted and
drew in other universities and religious orders as well as a widening lay
audience. The papacy proceeded against Luther cautiously at first, in part
because of the political aims of the pope, Leo X (r. 1513–1521), formerly
Giovanni de' Medici. Aware that the electors of the Holy Roman Empire
were about to elect a new king of the Germans, Leo X hoped to block the
likely election of the Habsburg candidate, Archduke Charles, and wanted
the support of the elector Frederick of Saxony, who was Luther's prince.
But in late 1519, Charles V was unanimously elected king and emperor.*

Hans J. Hillerbrand, ed. and trans., *The Reformation. A Narrative History Related by
Contemporary Observers and Participants* (London: SCM Press, 1964), 80–84.

The pope now moved more vigorously against Luther. The result was the following papal bull, which condemned Luther's theological errors, enumerated in forty-one articles, and threatened him with excommunication as a heretic.

Leo, Bishop, servant of the servants of God, to eternal memory. Arise, O Lord, and judge thy cause. Be mindful of the daily slander against thee by the foolish; incline thy ear to our supplication. Foxes have arisen which want to devastate thy vineyard, where thou hast worked the winepress. At thy ascension into heaven thou hast commanded the care, rule, and administration of this vineyard to Peter as head and to thy representatives, his successors, as the Church triumphant. A roaring sow of the woods had undertaken to destroy this vineyard; a wild beast wants to devour it.

Rise, O Peter, according to thy responsibility and care, bestowed upon thee by God. Be eagerly mindful of the cause of the holy Roman Church, mother of all churches and mistress of the faith, which thou hast sanctified according to God's commandment with thy blood and against which, as thou hast said, deceitful teachers have arisen, establishing sects and divisions. . . .

Finally, arise and lift yourself up, thou entire communion of the saints and thou entire Christian Church, whose truthful interpretation of the Sacred Scriptures is perturbed, some of whom the Father of Lies has blinded the senses so that they, according to the ancient custom of heretics, in their own wisdom, force, bend, and forge the Scriptures to have a meaning different than that dictated by the Holy Spirit. . . .

Reputable men have reported to us what we can hardly express without fearfulness and pain. We have unfortunately seen and read with our own eyes many and various errors, some of which have already been condemned by the councils and definitions of our predecessors, since they incorporate the heresies of the Greeks and the Bohemians. . . .

This we find all the more painful because our predecessors and we ourselves have always had a particular fondness for the German people. . . . The German people have truly been the friends of Christian truth and always the most serious opponents of heresy. This is shown by the commendable laws of the German emperors for the freedom of the Church and their laws always to suppress heretics from the German territory. If these laws were kept today we would not find ourselves in this difficult situation. . . . This is indeed shown by the German blood shed so often against the Bohemians. . . . Thus, prompted by the responsibility of our episcopal office, which is entrusted to us, we can no longer suffer the deadly poison of the described errors to lead to the diminishing of the Christian faith. Therefore we have enumerated some of these errors in this bull. . . .

1. It is a heretical opinion, but a common one, that the sacraments of the new law give pardoning grace to those who do not set up an obstacle.

2. To deny that in a child after baptism sin remains is to treat with contempt both Paul and Christ.

3. The inflammable sources of sin, even if there be no actual sin, delay a soul departing from the body from entrance into heaven. . . .

18. Indulgences are pious frauds of the faithful, and remissions of good works; and they are among those things which are allowed and those which are advantageous. . . .

20. They are led astray who believe that indulgences are salutary and useful for the fruit of the spirit. . . .

23. Excommunication is only an external penalty and does not deprive man of the common spiritual prayers of the Church.

24. Christians must be taught to cherish excommunications rather than to fear them.

25. The Roman Pontiff, the successor of Peter, is not the vicar of Christ over all the churches of the entire world, instituted by Christ himself in blessed Peter. . . .

27. It is certain that it is not in the power of the Church or the pope to establish articles of faith, much less laws concerning morals or good works. . . .

31. In every good work the righteous man sins.

32. A good work done very well is a venial sin.

33. To burn heretics is against the will of the Spirit.

34. To go to war against the Turks is to resist God, who punishes our iniquities through them.

35. No one is certain that he is not always sinning mortally, because of the truly hidden vice of pride.

36. Free will after sin is a matter of name only; and as long as one does what is in him, one sins mortally. . . .

41. Ecclesiastical prelates and secular rulers would not act badly if they would destroy all of the money bags of beggary.

Since these errors, as well as many others, are found in the writings or pamphlets of a certain Martin Luther, we condemn and reject and denounce these pamphlets and all writings and sermons of this Martin, be they in Latin or other languages, in which one or more of these errors are found. For all times do we want them condemned, rejected and denounced. We order in the name of the holy obedience and the danger of all punishment each and every Christian believer of either sex, under no circumstances to read, speak, preach, laud, consider, publish, or defend such writings, sermons, or broadsides or anything contained therein. . . .

Indeed, they are, upon learning of this bull, wherever they may be, to burn his writings, publically and in the presence of clerics and laity in order to avoid the punishment stated above. . . .

We prohibit this Martin from now on and henceforth to contrive any preaching or the office of preaching. And even though the love of righteousness and virtue did not take him away from sin and the hope of forgiveness did not lead him to penance, perhaps the terror of the pain of punishment may move him. Thus we beseech and remind this Martin, his supporters and accomplices of his holy orders and the described punishment. We ask him earnestly that he and his supporters, adherents and accomplices desist within sixty days . . . from preaching, both expounding their views and denouncing others, from publishing books and pamphlets concerning some or all of their errors. Furthermore, all writings which contain some or all of his errors are to be burned. Furthermore, this Martin is to recant perpetually such errors and views.

MARTIN LUTHER

To the Christian Nobility of the German Nation
1520

*In the second half of 1520 Luther wrote three powerful treatises that cata-
pulted him and the reform movement to great public attention. These
tracts, in chronological order, were* To the Christian Nobility of the German Nation concerning the Reform of the Christian Estate *(August),*
The Babylonian Captivity of the Church *(October), and* The Freedom
of a Christian *(November). Here, the first, written in the vernacular for
the laity, is briefly excerpted. The other two writings attacked the state
of the Roman church and expounded on Luther's concept of Christian
freedom as spiritual freedom from the law.*

*In his address to the nobility, Luther swiftly moved from the general
mood of German society's desperate need for reform to the reform of the
clergy, the spiritual estate. Arguing that the clergy were incapable of
reforming themselves and that, in a most stunning assertion, there was
no such thing as a separate clerical estate, Luther designated the nobility
as the logical group to take charge of reforming society. When he turned
his attention to secular affairs, he presented an odd laundry list of social
and economic reforms that he thought Germany needed. An amelioration
of the conditions facing the common people was not included on this list,
but the work showed that Luther did not confine his views on what needed
reform to religious and ecclesiastical affairs.*

---

*To His Most Illustrious, Most Mighty, and Imperial Majesty [Charles V],
and to the Christian Nobility of the German Nation, from Doctor Martin
Luther.* . . . All the estates of Christendom, particularly in Germany, are
now oppressed by distress and affliction, and this has stirred not only me
but everybody else to cry out time and time again and to pray for help. It
has even compelled me now at this time to cry aloud that God may inspire
someone with his Spirit to lend a helping hand to this distressed and
wretched nation. . . . [W]e must realize that in this matter [the reform

---

Martin Luther, *Luther's Works*, ed. Jaroslav Pelikan and Helmut T. Lehmann, trans.
Charles M. Jacobs, rev. James Atkinson (St. Louis: Concordia, 1955–), 44:123–217.

of the clergy] we are not dealing with men, but with the princes of hell. These [clerical] princes could fill the world with war and bloodshed, but war and bloodshed do not overcome them.[1] We must tackle this job by renouncing trust in physical force and trusting humbly in God. . . . Otherwise, we may start the game with great prospects of success, but when we get into it the evil spirits will stir up such confusion that the whole world will swim in blood, and then nothing will come of it all. Let us act wisely, therefore, and in the fear of God. The more force we use, the greater our disaster if we do not act humbly and in the fear of God. . . .

The Romanists have very cleverly built three walls around themselves. . . .

In the first place, when pressed by the temporal power they have made decrees and declared that the temporal power had no jurisdiction over them but that, on the contrary, the spiritual power is above the temporal. In the second place, when the attempt is made to reprove them with the Scriptures, they raise the objection that only the pope may interpret the Scriptures. In the third place, if threatened with a council, their story is that no one may summon a council but the pope. . . .

Let us begin by attacking the first wall. It is pure invention that pope, bishop, priests, and monks are called the spiritual estate while princes, lords, artisans, and farmers are called the temporal estate. This is indeed a piece of deceit and hypocrisy. Yet no one need be intimidated by it, and for this reason: all Christians are truly of the spiritual estate, and there is no difference among them except that of office. Paul says in 1 Corinthians 12[:12–13] that we are all one body, yet every member has its own work by which it serves the others. This is because we all have one baptism, one gospel, one faith, and are all Christians alike; for baptism, gospel and faith alone make us spiritual and a Christian people. . . .

[W]e are all consecrated priests through baptism. . . .

It follows from this argument that there is no true, basic difference between laymen and priests, princes and bishops, between religious and secular, except for the sake of office and work, but not for the sake of status. . . .

Therefore, just as those who are now called "spiritual," that is, priests, bishops, or popes, are neither different from other Christians nor superior to them, except that they are charged with the administration of the

---

[1] Ecclesiastical authorities in the Holy Roman Empire occupied a unique position in Europe in that many of them also held the rank of princes of the empire and exercised secular as well as spiritual authority. See Map 1.

Word of God and the sacraments, which is their work and office, so it is with the temporal authorities. They bear the sword and rod in their hand to punish the wicked and protect the good. . . .

I say therefore that since the temporal power is ordained of God to punish the wicked and protect the good, it should be left free to perform its office in the whole body of Christendom without restriction and without respect to persons, whether it affects pope, bishops, priests, monks, nuns, or anyone else. . . .

The second wall is still more loosely built and less substantial. The Romanists want to be the only masters of Holy Scripture, although they never learn a thing from the Bible all their life long. . . .

[T]heir claim that only the pope may interpret Scripture is an outrageous fancied fable. They cannot produce a single letter [of Scripture] to maintain that the interpretation of Scripture or the confirmation of its interpretation belongs to the pope alone. They themselves have usurped this power. . . .

The third wall falls of itself when the first two are down. When the pope acts contrary to the Scriptures, it is our duty to stand by the Scriptures, to reprove him and to constrain him. . . .

The Romanists have no basis in Scripture for their claim that the Pope alone has the right to call or confirm a council. . . .

Therefore, when necessity demands it, and the pope is an offense to Christendom, the first man who is able should, as a true member of the whole body, do what he can to bring about a truly free council. No one can do this so well as the temporal authorities, especially since they are also fellow-Christians, fellow-priests, fellow-members of the spiritual estate, and fellow-lords over all things. . . .

We shall now look at the matters which ought to be properly dealt with in councils, matters with which popes, cardinals, bishops, and all scholars ought properly to be occupied day and night if they loved Christ and his church. But if this is not the case, let ordinary people and the temporal authorities do it without regard to papal bans and fulminations.[2] . . .

[The tract then listed a lengthy series of abuses and failings in the Roman church and the clergy, ranging from the lavish and ostentatious lifestyle of the pope to parasitical cardinals at an overcrowded papal court, and from the excessive number of feast days to the scholastic curriculum of

---

[2] Luther at this point explicitly authorized the common people as well as secular ruling elites to take action to bring about reform in the church.

the universities. All this, according to Luther, required an immediate
reformation. At the conclusion of the tract, Luther turned his attention to
secular matters that also needed reform:]

Enough has now been said about the failings of the clergy, though you may find more and will find more if you look in the right place. We shall now devote a section to the failings of the temporal estate.

In the first place, there is a great need for a general law and decree in the German nation against extravagant and costly dress, because of which so many nobles and rich men are impoverished. . . .

It is also necessary to restrict the spice traffic, which is another of the great ships in which money is carried out of German lands. By the grace of God, more things to eat and drink grow in our own land than in any other, and they are just as nourishing and good. . . .

But the greatest misfortune of the German nation is certainly the [purchase of annuities].[3] If that did not exist many a man would have to leave unbought his silks, velvets, golden ornaments, spices, and display of every kind. This traffic has not existed much longer than a hundred years, and it has already brought almost all princes, endowed institutions, cities, nobles, and their heirs to poverty, misery, and ruin. . . .

In this connection, we must put a bit in the mouth of the Fuggers and similar companies.[4] How is it possible in the lifetime of one man to accumulate such great possessions, worthy of a king, legally and according to God's will? I don't know. But what I really cannot understand is how a man with one hundred gulden can make a profit of twenty in one year. Nor, for that matter, can I understand how a man with one gulden can make another—and all this is not from tilling the soil or raising cattle, where the increase of wealth depends not on human wit but on God's blessing. . . .

Next comes the abuse of eating and drinking, which gives us Germans a bad reputation in foreign lands, as though it were a special vice of ours. Preaching cannot stop it, so deeply is it rooted and so firmly has it got the upper hand. The waste of money would be its least evil, were it not followed by all the vices that accompany it—murder, adultery, stealing,

---

[3] *zynskauf.* Investors purchased annuities by making a one-time payment and in exchange receiving a guaranteed annual payment, normally a fixed percentage of the original investment, for the life of the annuity holder.

[4] The Fugger firm of Augsburg was the most highly capitalized company in Europe in the early sixteenth century. Other important merchant firms in Augsburg included the Welsers and Hochstetters.

blasphemy, and every other form of immorality. Government can do something to prevent it. . . .

Finally, is it not lamentable that we Christians tolerate open and common brothels in our midst, when all of us are baptized unto chastity? I know perfectly well what some say to this, that is, that it is not a custom peculiar to one nation, that it would be difficult to put a stop to it, and, moreover, that it is better to keep such houses than that married women, or girls, or others of still more honorable estate should be outraged [by harassment, assault, and rape]. Nevertheless, should not the government, which is temporal and also Christian, realize that such evil cannot be prevented by that kind of heathenish practice? . . .

In this matter of brothels, and in other matters previously mentioned, I have tried to point out how many good works the temporal government could do, and what the duty of every government should be, so that everyone may learn what an awful responsibility it is to rule and sit in high places. . . . It is the duty of authorities to seek the best for those they govern. . . .

Much more could be said of this pitiable state of affairs. . . . They want to exercise authority far and wide, and yet they help nobody. For just this reason a lord and ruler will be a rare sight in heaven, even though he build a hundred churches for God and raise up all the dead! . . .

God give us all a Christian mind, and grant to the Christian nobility of the German nation in particular true spiritual courage to do the best they can for the poor church. Amen.

Wittenberg, in the year 1520.

7

Greasing the Bundschuh

1522

This woodcut illustration is taken from a 1522 pamphlet by one of Luther's most determined Roman Catholic opponents, Thomas Murner. The pamphlet, entitled About the Great Lutheran Fool, *sought to make clear the social and political as well as religious dangers inherent in Luther's teachings. The illustration by an unknown artist, entitled* Greasing the Bundschuh (Den buntschuch schmieren), *bore the subtitle "How Luther greases the Bundschuh so that he remains pleasing to the simple man." The German word* schmieren *means to bribe as well as to grease. The woodcut thus associated Luther, dressed in armor as a knight and prepared for war, with the Bundschuh, the symbol of pre-Reformation peasant insurrection in the Upper Rhine (Document 1). The peasant's bound leather shoe needed to be greased to make it waterproof, and by heating the leather in a fire, the grease could penetrate the leather more thoroughly. The message of the illustration, in short, was "Luther's teachings promote rebellion."*

Den buntschuch schmieren.

Wie der luther den buntschůch schmiert/ das er den
einfaltigen menschen angenem bleib.

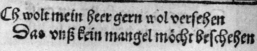

Eß wolt mein herr gern wol versehen
Das vnß kein mangel möcht beschehen

56

MARTIN LUTHER

A Sincere Admonition to Guard against Rebellion
1522

---

*In 1522, following anticlerical and iconoclastic violence at Wittenberg,
Luther wrote to his followers urging them to avoid rebellion. In Luther's
view, popular hostility was directed against only the clergy, who richly
deserved this hatred and for whom insurrection would, in fact, be too
mild a punishment. But Luther asserted in his* A Sincere Admonition
by Martin Luther to all Christians to Guard against Insurrection and
Rebellion *that commoners should only act against the church at the
command or with the authorization of the nobles and princes, who by
definition could not be rebellious. The tract revealed not only that Luther
did not foresee a rebellion but also that at an early date he was funda-
mentally opposed to an insurrection by the common people, which he
saw as unjust, impractical, and diabolical. Already in his address* To
the Christian Nobility of the German Nation *(Document 6) Luther had
cautioned that the Reformation movement needed to trust in God and not
in physical force.*

May God grant grace and peace to all Christians who read this pamphlet
or hear it read.

By the grace of God, the blessed light of Christian truth, hitherto
suppressed by the pope and his adherents, has risen again in our day.
Their manifold harmful and scandalous deceits and all manner of misdeeds and tyranny have thereby been publicly exposed and brought to
shame. It seems likely that this may result in an insurrection, and that
priests, monks, bishops, and the entire clerical estate may be murdered
or driven into exile unless they themselves demonstrate some serious
and significant improvement. For the common man seems to be discontented and brooding over the damage he has suffered in property,
body, and soul. Apparently they have tried him too far, with utter lack

---

Martin Luther, *Luther's Works*, ed. Jaroslav Pelikan and Helmut T. Lehmann, trans.
W. A. Lambert, rev. Walther I. Brandt (St. Louis: Concordia, 1955–), 45:57–74.

of scruple, burdening him beyond all measure. He seems to be neither able nor willing to endure it any longer, and to have good reason to lay about him with flail and cudgel. . . .

I am not at all displeased to hear that the clergy are in such a state of fear and anxiety; perhaps they will come to their senses and moderate their mad tyranny. Would to God that their terror and fear were even greater! Nevertheless, I think—indeed I am sure and have no fear whatever on this score—that there will not be any insurrection or rebellion. . . .

Their [the clergy's] wickedness is so horrible that no punishment is adequate except the wrath of God itself, without any intermediary. For this reason I have never yet let men persuade me to oppose those who threaten to use fist and flail; I know full well that they will never get that far. Even if a few [clerics] should get roughed up, there will be no general resort to violence. . . .

Although the hand, therefore, will not get far, and there is, hence, no need for me to restrain it, I must nevertheless instruct men's hearts a little. As regards the hand, I leave matters to the temporal authorities and nobility. They should, of course, take action, each prince and lord in his own territory, by virtue of the obligations incumbent upon such duly constituted authority; for what is done by duly constituted authority cannot be regarded as insurrection. . . . But we must calm the mind of the common man, and tell him to abstain from the words and even the passions which lead to insurrection, and to do nothing in the matter apart from a command of his superiors or an action of the authorities. . . .

For insurrection lacks discernment; it generally harms the innocent more than the guilty. Hence, no insurrection is ever right, no matter how right the cause it seeks to promote. It always results in more damage than improvement. . . . I am and always will be on the side of those against whom insurrection is directed, no matter how unjust their cause. . . .

Now insurrection is nothing else than being one's own judge and avenger, and that is something God cannot tolerate. . . . God is not on the side of insurrection.

[I]n this particular case insurrection is most certainly a suggestion of the Devil. He sees the bright light of the truth exposing his idols, the pope and the papists, before all the world and he simply cannot cope with it. Its brilliant rays have so dazzled his eyes and blinded him that he can do nothing more than lie, blaspheme, and suggest errant nonsense. He even forgets to assume the hypocritical appearance of respectability. . . .

Therefore, there is no need for you to demand an armed insurrection. Christ himself has already begun an insurrection with his mouth, one which will be more than the pope can bear. Let us follow that one, and carry on.

9

Peasants Torturing an Indulgence Preacher

1525

This pen and ink drawing was an illustration for a 1525 Shrove Tuesday play, The Indulgence Seller *(Der Ablasskrämer), by the Swiss author Niklaus Manuel Deutsch. The image depicted a group of peasants torturing the indulgence preacher Richard Hinterlist, whose last name means "fraud" and hence who may have been a mythical or symbolical figure. Despite the Reformation's potentially adverse impact on their professional careers—it would result in a decline of ecclesiastical patronage for works of art—many artists of the northern Renaissance supported the Reformation.*

The image, which gives the preacher's name above his head, reveals the active role that women sometimes played in popular disturbances. The peasant woman on the left side of the image holds a rolled document, perhaps a letter of indulgence, in her left hand and a weapon in her right hand. The woman beneath Hinterlist is pulling on the weight tied to his feet in order to produce added pain in his shoulder joints. The punishment the peasants inflicted was the strappado, a standard early-modern form of torture, which remained common into the modern era.

The fate that the indulgence preacher Hinterlist suffered shows why the evangelical movement in the early 1520s aroused the kind of fear in the clergy that Luther said (in Document 8) they had coming. The drawing also suggests something of the anticlerical rage that commoners felt in the early years of the Reformation against those whom they felt had defrauded them. The irony is that just a few years previously, these peasants might have been eager purchasers of indulgence letters.

Der Ablasskraemer. Burgerbibliothek Bern, Mss.h.h.XVI.159, f. 2r.

indulgences scrolls

10

HULDRYCH ZWINGLI

The Sixty-Seven Articles
1523

In addition to Luther's Wittenberg, another influential center of the early Reformation was the Swiss city of Zurich, where from the early 1520s Huldrych Zwingli preached about the need for reformation. The extent to which Luther influenced Zwingli is debated. In 1523, Zwingli laid out his reform program in a series of sixty-seven articles, which he framed for debate with a Catholic representative of the bishop of Constance. By this time, he had come to differ from Luther on several key issues, including the role of secular government in ecclesiastical affairs and the need for secular law to embody the law of God. Unlike Luther's equivocating stance—sometimes calling for secular authorities to effect a Reformation in the church, sometimes insisting they had no right to act in spiritual matters—Zwingli advocated a close alliance of political authorities and the clergy. In the following articles, Zwingli developed his thought concerning the Christian's obligation of obedience to secular authority and the right of resistance, the authority's obligation to rule in a Christian manner, and the Christian's right to depose an authority who violated divine law. The articles also show (as did Document 7) that some Roman Catholic authorities linked Luther's reforms and the Bundschuh movement of the peasants.

The Thirty-Eighth Article

All Christians without exception owe obedience to [the secular authorities], provided they do not command anything which is opposed to God.

This article limits the tyranny of superiors, so that they might not begin to act irrationally and wantonly, just because God ordered that we be obedient to them. . . .

Therefore, good Christians, when princes dare forbid you the teaching of Christ so that you neither hear, nor read nor preach the same, pay

Huldrych Zwingli, *Writings*, vol. 1, *The Defense of the Reformed Faith*, trans. E. J. Furcha (Allison Park, Pa.: Pickwick Publications, 1984), 260–82.

no heed to them. You say, "but what if they kill me?" . . . You ought to rejoice that God uses your life and blood in order to water and increase his word. For what use is your blood when it decays and spoils in your dying body, Ps. 29 [30:10]? Is it not better to be poured out as a fertilizer of the word of God?

You see how the foolish princes have allowed themselves to be misled by the anti-Christian papists, so that some time ago they persecuted the gospel of Christ in Luther's name by calling the teaching of Christ from that time on Lutheran, by whom, after all, it was proclaimed, and by persecuting it to the best of their ability.[1] And when one pays little attention to this (for everyone well knows within himself how he has to become a believer), they begin to call the teaching of Christ a conspiracy [*Bundschuh*], so that they may be the more justified in the eyes of people, should they undertake to eradicate the teaching of Christ by murdering. . . .

Should things go on as they are now, you [unrighteous princes] will experience in your own skin what you inflict upon the skin of others. If you use force, force will be used on you; for with whatever measure you mete out, with that same measure things shall be meted out to you [Mk. 4:24]. . . .

The Thirty-Ninth Article

Therefore all [secular rulers'] laws ought to conform to the divine will so that they protect the oppressed person, though he may not actually lay a charge [against anyone].

Should the laws of the princes be against God, then Christians will say, as we heard earlier, that one ought to obey God more than people [Acts 5:29]. Christian princes ought to have laws, therefore, which are not opposed to God, or else one might evade them, which brings unrest in its wake. . . .

Though you do well in protecting the righteous and though this is your duty, as we shall show later, it is, nonetheless, the wicked ones who are the reason we have to support you, so that the righteous people may

---

[1] Zwingli is apparently referring to the prohibition, ordered by some Catholic princes, against Luther's translation of the New Testament, which was published in 1522. Luther responded to this prohibition, like Zwingli, by declaring that such an edict need not be complied with, that is, by authorizing passive resistance against secular authorities who commanded what they had no right to order. Zwingli noted that these authorities then charged Luther (and Christ's teachings) with treasonous conspiracy, that is, with seeking to foment a Bundschuh.

be protected from them. Which righteous people? Is there one among you who is righteous from within? No. You can protect only those who have not done wrong in outward deeds; inwardly they, too, are full of temptation. Thus you rule only among God's knaves and you yourself are one. Here I call anyone a knave of God who is not righteous before God. In other words, all persons are knaves of God, for all persons are sinners. The only thing you are able to stop is that excessive wickedness is not committed. . . .

The Fortieth Article

[Magistrates] alone are entitled to impose the death penalty and then only on those who give public offense, without thereby incurring the wrath of God. . . .

The Forty-First Article

When [rulers] provide just counsel and aid to those for whom they will have to give account before God, these in turn, are duty-bound to give them physical support.

Everyone understands what this article aims at, namely, that rulers who carry out the office entrusted to them, which is to administer justice, advise the simple and keep him from despair, help the weak and not allow him to be oppressed, to manage according to necessity and in earnest, are then also entitled to have their expended time and the neglect of their own affairs restored by those who thus receive their help and use it, provided, of course, that they suffered loss from this which they cannot easily absorb. . . .

At times you find a semblance of this among councilors in cities and towns, but not too often among the ruling nobility; these, be they ever so rich, do not make any concessions to the poor; by that much less are they like God. Of course, they are entitled within reasonable limits to collect their due according to human justice. . . .

In this connection we ought not to forget the despots either, of whom unfortunately there are as many as there are fleas in August. . . . For so many of the temporal rulers have now gone astray that every sensible person can readily see that it would be much better were they not in office at all since they carry it out in such an inhuman manner. And there are those who impose new taxes on their people without their approval, but by sheer force. . . . And they allow such heavy burdens to come upon their people in order that they, too, might get a share. Because of this they tolerate holders of monopolies among them which, according to their laws, are prohibited to operate. One has to buy spices, zinc, copper, cloth and articles of clothing from these holders of monopolies. These burden not only a princedom, but indeed the entire world. . . .

The Forty-Second Article

Should [rulers] become unfaithful and not act according to the precepts of Christ, they may be deposed in the name of God. . . .

[O]ne who fails to punish the sinner does not follow the precepts of Christ, but actually favors him and oppresses the innocent. This is when one protects useless bellies, lazy priests, monks and nuns in their wantonness, their adultery, chess games, greed, pride and pomp. And what they squander, they do not allocate to the poor. Rather, when one speaks truthfully against all this, they punish the one who objects. This certainly is to be outside the precepts of Christ.

But they should be deposed in such cases, as is shown by the clear example of Saul, whom God rejected though he had earlier chosen him, 1 Kings 15 & 16 (1 Sam. 15 & 16). Indeed, should one fail to depose extravagant kings, the entire people will be penalized on their account, Jer. 15:4. . . . In short, had the Jews not allowed their king to carry out uncensored wantonness, God would not have punished them. One must pluck out the eye, if it offends and throw it away, and cut off the hand or the foot [cf. Mt. 18:8ff].

How one is to depose the same, may be readily noted. It is not to be done with killing, war and rioting, but in a different manner altogether; for God has called us to peace, 1 Cor. 7:15.

[If] the king or lord [is] elected by the common people and should he commit a crime, then the people are also to depose him; failing this they will be punished with him.

And if a small number of princes elected him, one is to report to the princes that his offensive life can no longer be tolerated and he should be ordered deposed. . . .

Now should the despot not have been elected by anyone and, instead, have inherited the kingdom, I do not know how such a kingdom is to have any foundation at all. Then treat the born king as if he were a fool or a child. You still have to accept him as lord. But how is he to rule? It follows then, not as the popular saying goes, that a king's son is either a fool or a king, but rather that he is both at once: a fool and a king. The kingdom will have to be governed by other wise persons. It would be simpler therefore to make a wise person king; for it is an unfortunate and cursed land, indeed, whose king is a child [Eccl. 10:16]. Those who define the term "despot" say that a despot is one who rules on the basis of his own power and ambition. Thus I do not know where the idea of inheriting a kingdom came from, unless it be by the common agreement and consent of the people. But though such a one turns out to be a tyrant, not just anyone is entitled to depose him; for that leads to rebellion only, whereas the kingdom of God is justice, peace and joy in the Holy Spirit, Rom. 14:17. But when the entire populace is united in deposing the despot because he acts against God, then it is with God (or at least, in large measure), so that a rebellion may be prevented thereby. Thus, had the children of Israel deposed Manasseh in that manner, God would not have punished them along with him [2 Kings 21]. You say, when does it ever happen that the larger God-fearing part of the nation is one? Answer: When there is no unanimity I say, once again, that you ought to bear the yoke of the despot and when you are punished with him in the end, do not complain. . . .

There is no lack of counsel or of ways to depose the despots: what is lacking is common piety. Take heed, you tyrants. The gospel shall raise up righteous people. Become righteous too, and you will be borne up on hands. But should you fail to do so and acquire unjust goods by force, you will be trampled under foot.

11

MARTIN LUTHER

The Rights of a Christian Congregation
1523

By 1523, Luther doubted that the nobility was the proper agency to bring about reform, a departure from the position he had expressed in 1520 (Document 6). The shift was especially due to princes, loyal to Rome, who prohibited their subjects from possessing his translation of the New Testament. This led Luther to argue that secular rulers had no competence when it came to spiritual matters and that subjects should engage in

Martin Luther, *Luther's Works*, ed. Jaroslav Pelikan and Helmut T. Lehmann, trans. Eric W. and Ruth C. Gritsch (St. Louis: Concordia, 1955–), 39:306–14.

passive resistance if their rulers' commands violated divine law. Also in 1523, Luther wrote a tract encouraging congregationally or communally based reformation and giving the local Christian community wide-ranging powers to determine its own religious life. In this work (entitled That a Christian Assembly or Congregation Has the Right and Power to Judge All Teaching and to Call, Appoint and Dismiss Teachers, Established and Proved by Scripture, *excerpted here), he laid down two basic programmatic principles for a Reformation centered on the local congregation or community—what historians refer to as the "communal Reformation." First, he granted to each local assembly of Christians the right to determine for itself the doctrines that it would accept and put into practice in members' lives. Second, in developing what was implied in this first principle, Luther also granted to the local community of Christians the right to choose its own minister or teacher. If the congregation disagreed with its minister about the content of gospel, it had the right to dismiss the minister and to engage another. These two principles were fundamental demands of the commoners during the Peasants' War, often set forth at the very beginning of their programs.*

First, it is necessary to know where and what the Christian congregation is, so that men do not engage in human affairs (as the non-Christians were accustomed to do) in the name of the Christian congregation. The sure mark by which the Christian congregation can be recognized is that the pure gospel is preached there. For just as the banner of an army is the sure sign by which one can know what kind of lord and army have taken to the field, so, too, the gospel is the sure sign by which one knows where Christ and his army are encamped. . . .

Thus it undeniably follows that bishops, religious foundations, monasteries, and all who are associated with them have long since ceased to be Christians or Christian congregations. . . .

Second, in this matter of judging teachings and appointing or dismissing teachers or pastors, one should not care at all about human statutes, law, old precedent, usage, custom, etc., even if they were instituted by pope or emperor, prince or bishop, if one half or the whole world accepted them, or if they lasted one year or a thousand years. For the soul of man is something eternal, and more important than every temporal thing. . . .

[Christ] takes both the right and the power to judge teaching from the bishops, scholars, and councils and gives them to everyone and to all Christians equally when he says, John 10[:4], "My sheep know my voice." Again, "My sheep do not follow strangers, but flee from them, for they do not know the voice of strangers" [John 10:5]. Again, "No matter how many of them have come, they are thieves and murderers. But the sheep did not listen to them" [John 10:8]. . . .

[Papal authorities] shamelessly take away the judgment of teaching from the sheep and annex it to themselves through their own law and blasphemy. That is why they should certainly be regarded as murderers and thieves, as wolves and apostate Christians, for they are openly convicted here not only of denying God's word but also of opposing and acting against it. Such action was quite appropriate for the Antichrist and his kingdom, according to the prophecy of St. Paul, II Thessalonians 2[:3–4]. . . .

Thus we conclude that wherever there is a Christian congregation in possession of the gospel, it not only has the right and power but also the duty—on pain of losing the salvation of its souls and in accordance with the promise made to Christ in baptism—to avoid, to flee, to depose, and to withdraw from the authority that our bishops, abbots, monasteries, religious foundations, and the like are now exercising. For it is clearly evident that they teach and rule contrary to God and his word. . . .

Second, since a Christian congregation neither should nor could exist without God's word, it clearly follows from the previous [argument] that it nevertheless must have teachers and preachers who administer the word. And since in these last accursed times the bishops and the false spiritual government neither are nor wish to be teachers—moreover, they want neither to prove nor to tolerate any, and God should not be tempted to send new preachers from heaven—we must act according to Scripture and call and institute from among ourselves those who are found to be qualified and whom God has enlightened with reason and endowed with gifts to do so. . . .

Thus I ask the dear tyrants: if bishops are made by the election and call of their congregation, and if the pope is pope without confirmation by any other authority and by election alone, why should not a Christian congregation, too, make a preacher by its call alone? For they [the tyrants] regard the episcopal and papal estate as higher than the office of preaching! Who gave them this right and took it from us, especially since our calling has Scripture on its side, but their calling is nothing but a mere human trifle without Scripture, with which they rob us of our rights? They are tyrants and knaves who deal with us just as the devil's apostles should. . . .

Therefore, whoever has the office of preaching imposed on him has the highest office in Christendom imposed on him. Afterward he may also baptize, celebrate mass, and exercise all pastoral care; or, if he does not wish to do so, he may confine himself to preaching and leave baptizing and other lower offices to others—as Christ and all apostles did, Acts 4 [6:4]. Thus it becomes evident that our present-day bishops are spiritual idols and not bishops. For they leave the highest office of the word, which should be their own, in the hands of the very lowest [orders], namely, chaplains, monks, and mendicants. They also leave the lower offices such as baptizing and pastoral care to them. In the meantime, however, they administer confirmation, consecrate bells, altars, and churches which are neither Christian nor episcopal duties and which they themselves invented. They are perverted and blind masks and true child-bishops.

12

THOMAS MÜNTZER

Sermon to the Princes

1524

Thomas Müntzer, an independent-minded radical reformer, was with Luther at Wittenberg at the start of the Reformation but later broke with him and became one of Luther's sharpest critics within the camp of the evangelical reformers. From Easter 1523, Müntzer was pastor at the small market town of Allstedt, where he developed his own distinctive reform program. He composed the first vernacular liturgy of the German Reformation, and this liturgy and his sermons gained the support of people in Allstedt and neighboring villages. Müntzer also formed a secret group of his followers, the League of the Elect. In April 1524, this group burned down a shrine dedicated to the Blessed Virgin that belonged to a local convent, to which Allstedters owed dues.

When Catholic nobles in the region sought to prohibit their subjects from attending Müntzer's services, he seized the opportunity to preach a

Michael G. Baylor, ed. and trans., *The Radical Reformation* (Cambridge: Cambridge University Press, 1991), 11–32.

sermon to the visiting duke John of Saxony, Crown Prince John Frederick, and other officials of electoral Saxony. Using a biblical text about Daniel, an Old Testament prophet who became the adviser of King Nebuchadnezzar, Müntzer offered himself to the Saxon princes as a "new Daniel." He used the sermon to expound his views on the revelatory potential of certain dreams and the arrival of the apocalyptical "last days." Like Zwingli, he insisted that rulers had Christian duties to fulfill, including using their power to protect the pious and destroy the godless. More forcefully than Zwingli, Müntzer also issued a warning: If the princes of Saxony did not act as they should, they would lose "the sword"—the power of government. Shortly after he delivered the sermon on July 13, 1524, Müntzer's Allstedt printer published an extended version, which is excerpted here.

An exposition of the second chapter of Daniel the prophet, preached at the castle of Allstedt before the active and dear dukes and rulers of Saxony by Thomas Müntzer, servant of the Word of God.

Allstedt, 1524.

It is to be understood that poor, miserable, disintegrating Christendom can neither be counseled nor assisted unless diligent, indefatigable servants of God promote the Bible daily by reciting, reading and preaching. But if this is done, the head of many a pampered cleric must either suffer a continuous rain of hard blows or he will have to give up his profession. How can this be avoided when Christendom is being so terribly devastated by ravaging wolves? . . .

[W]hoever is inexperienced and an enemy of visions due to a carnal consciousness, and either accepts them all without any discrimination or rejects them all because the false dream interpreters of the world have done such harm by being greedy and selfish, this person will not fare well. . . . For God clearly speaks, as in this text of Daniel, about the transformation of the world.[1] He will bring about this transformation in the Last Days, so that his name will be rightly praised. He will release the elect from their shame and pour forth his spirit over all flesh. And our sons and daughters shall prophesy and shall have dreams and visions,

---

[1] The text of Daniel 2 describes a dream image of King Nebuchadnezzar, which Daniel, unlike the king's soothsayers, is able to describe. The image in the king's dream was a statue, with various parts composed of various metals. Müntzer's use of this figure as a symbol of the five ages of history was conventional in Christian biblical interpretation. What was unique was the political message for his own time that Müntzer drew from this interpretation.

etc. For if Christendom is not to become apostolic, Acts 27[2] where Joel is cited, why then should one preach? To what purpose then are visions in the Bible?

It is true — and I know it to be true — that the spirit of God now reveals to many elected, pious people that a momentous, invincible, future reformation is very necessary and must be brought about. Each one may protect himself against it as he wishes and yet the prophecy of Daniel remains undiminished, though no one believes it, as Paul also says to the Romans 3[:3]. This text of Daniel is thus as clear as the bright sun, and the work of ending the fifth empire of the world is now in full swing.

The first empire was symbolized by the golden head [of the statue in Nebuchadnezzar's dream]. That was the empire of Babylon. And the second empire was represented by the silver breast and arms, which was the empire of the Medes and Persians. The third empire was the empire of the Greeks, which resounded with its cleverness, indicated by the brass. The fourth empire was the Roman empire, which was won with the iron sword and was an empire of coercion. The fifth empire or monarchy is that which we have before our own eyes [i.e., the Holy Roman Empire] and it is also (like the fourth) of iron and would like to be coercive. But, as we see before our very eyes, the iron is intermixed with filth,[3] vain schemes of flattery that slither and squirm over the face of the whole earth. For he who cannot be a cheat [in our empire] must be an idiot. One sees now how prettily the eels and snakes copulate together in a heap. The priests and all the evil clergy are the snakes, as John the Baptist calls them, Matthew 3[:7], and the temporal lords and rulers are the eels, as is symbolized by the fish in Leviticus 11[:10–12]. For the Devil's empire has painted its face with clay.

Oh, you beloved lords, how well the Lord will smash down the old pots of clay [the ecclesiastical authorities] with his rod of iron, Psalm 2[:9]. Therefore, you most true and beloved regents, learn your knowledge directly from the mouth of God and do not let yourselves be seduced by your flattering priests and restrained by false patience and indulgence. For the stone [Christ's spirit] torn from the mountain without human touch has become great. The poor laity and the peasants see it much more clearly than you do. Yes, God be praised, the stone has become so

---

[2] Rather, Acts 2:16ff.

[3] That is, the Holy Roman Empire, like the Roman empire before it, is essentially a coercive apparatus of iron; but now the coercion is blunted and disguised by the intermixture of supposedly Christian spiritual elements. The combination of the two is symbolized for Müntzer by the feet of the statue in Nebuchadnezzar's dream (Dan. 2:41), which were of iron and clay. The clay is intensified by Müntzer to "filth."

great that already, if other lords or neighbors want to persecute you on account of the gospel, they would be overthrown by their own subjects. This I know to be true. Indeed the stone is great! The foolish world has long feared it. The stone fell upon the world when it was still small. What then should we do now, after it has grown so great and powerful? And after it has struck the great statue so powerfully and irresistibly that it has smashed down the old pots of clay?

Therefore, you dear rulers of Saxony, stand boldly on the cornerstone. . . . For God stands so close to you that you do not believe it. Why do you want to be frightened by the specter of man, Psalm 118[:6]?

Look closely at this text of Daniel! King Nebuchadnezzar wanted to kill the clever ones because they could not interpret the dream for him. This was deserved. For with their cleverness they wanted to rule his whole kingdom, and yet they could not even do what they had been engaged for. So also are our clergy today. . . .

Therefore a new Daniel must arise and interpret your revelation for you. And this same new Daniel must go forth, as Moses teaches, Deuteronomy 20, at the head of the troops. He must reconcile the anger of the princes and that of the enraged people. For if you were truly to experience the shame of Christendom and the deception of the false clergy and incorrigible rogues, then no one could imagine how enraged at them you would become. . . . For they have made fools of you, so that everyone now swears to the saints that princes are heathen people insofar as their office is concerned. Princes, they say, should do nothing but maintain civil unity.[4]

Oh, beloved ones, the great stone will indeed soon fall on and smite this view of your office and smash such rational schemes to the ground. For Christ says, in Matthew 10[:34], "I have not come to bring peace but the sword." But what should one do with these false spiritual leaders? Nothing but what is done with evildoers who obstruct the gospel: put them away and cut them off, if you do not want to be servants of the devil but servants of God, as Paul calls you in Romans 13[:14]. You should not doubt that God will smash to bits all your adversaries who undertake to persecute you. . . . Thus, you rulers are angels when you seek to act justly, as Peter says in 2 Peter 1[:4]. Christ commanded this

---

[4] A reference to Luther's doctrine of two "kingdoms" or "realms," the spiritual and the secular, according to which there is nothing specifically spiritual or Christian about secular political authority. In *On Secular Authority* (1523), Luther asserted that secular authority has no claim to rule over matters that concern the spirit, a view that conflicted with the argument in his *Address to the Christian Nobility of the German Nation* (Document 6).

very earnestly, Luke 19[:27], and said, "Take my enemies and strangle them for me before my eyes." Why? Ah, because they have spoiled Christ's government, and in addition they seek to defend their villainy under the guise of the Christian faith. And with their deceitful infamy they pollute the whole world. Therefore Christ our Lord says, Matthew 18[:6], "Whosoever does evil to one of these little ones, it is better for him that a millstone be hung about his neck and that he be thrown into the depths of the sea." He who wishes, twisting and turning here and there, can gloss over this. But these are the words of Christ. Now, if Christ can say this about someone who does evil to one of the little ones, what should be said about those who do evil to a great multitude in their faith? For this is how arch-villains act, who do evil to the whole world and make it deviate from the true Christian faith, and who say that no one shall know the mysteries of God. . . .

Now, should you want to be true rulers, then you must begin government at the roots, as Christ commanded. Drive his enemies away from the elect, for that is your appointed task. Beloved ones, do not offer us any stale posturing about how the power of God should do it without your application of the sword. Otherwise, may the sword rust away in its scabbard on you. May God grant this! . . .

Therefore do not permit evildoers who turn us away from God to live longer, Deuteronomy 13[:6]. For a godless person has no right to life when he hinders the pious. . . .

But for this use of the sword to occur as it should and in the right manner, our dear fathers who confess Christ with us—that is, the princes—should do it. But if they do not do it, then the sword will be taken away from them, Daniel 7[:27]. For then they confess Christ with words and deny him in their actions, Titus 1[:16]. Thus the princes should offer peace to the enemy, Deuteronomy 2[:26–30]. But if the princes want to be "spiritual" and not render an account of their knowledge of God, 1 Peter 3[:12–17], they should be gotten rid of, 1 Corinthians 5[:13]. I, together with pious Daniel, bid them not to oppose God's revelation. But if they do take the contrary course, may they be strangled without any mercy, as Hezekiah [2 Kg. 18:22], Josiah [2 Kg. 23:5], Cyrus [2 Chr. 36:22f.], Daniel [Dan. 6:27], and Elijah, I Kings 18[:40] destroyed the priests of Baal. Otherwise, the Christian church will not be able to return to its source. The tares must be pulled out of the vineyard of God at the time of the harvest. Then the beautiful golden wheat will gain lasting roots and come up right, Matthew 13[:24–30, 39]. The angels who sharpen their sickles for the cutting are the earnest servants of God who fulfill the zeal of divine wisdom, Malachi 3[:1–6]. . . .

In order that the truth may really be brought to light, you rulers—God grant that you do not willingly do otherwise—must act according to the conclusion of this chapter of Daniel. . . . That is, Nebuchadnezzar elevated holy Daniel to office so that the king might carry out good, correct decisions, inspired by the holy spirit. . . . For the godless have no right to life except that which the elect decide to grant them, as is written in the book of Exodus 23[:29–33]. Rejoice, you true friends of God, that the enemies of the cross have crapped their courage into their pants. They act righteously, even though they never once dreamed of doing so. If we now fear only God, why should we recoil before vacillating, incapable men, Numbers 14[:8f.], Joshua 11[:6]. Only be bold! He to whom is given all power in heaven and on earth [Christ] wants to lead the government, Matthew 28[:18]. To you, most beloved, may God grant eternal protection. Amen.

3

Religion and Politics in the Peasants' War

13

Articles of the Peasants of Stühlingen
Early 1525

*Historians commonly ascribe the start of the Peasants' War to distur-
bances that began in the small Black Forest territory of Stühlingen in
June 1524. The peasants there refused to fulfill obligations that they
regarded as unfair, and their protest set off a widening series of rebellions over the next months. The articles expressing their grievances were
drawn up later to support their case against their lords, which the peasants brought before an imperial court. The following excerpt from their
sixty-two articles shows that, while most of their grievances concerned
economic issues and were based on what they insisted were violations of
traditional customs in their lordship, they also opposed the institution of
serfdom on religious grounds. Several of the articles concerned the disabilities serfdom imposed, and they wanted serfdom to be abolished.*

1. The territories of Stühlingen and Lupfen demand that no one
   who has a fixed place of residence shall be imprisoned in civil
   causes.
2. Those arrested for criminal deeds should only be brought to
   justice before the court of the jurisdiction under which they
   reside or to which they are accountable.

Tom Scott and Bob Scribner, eds. and trans., *The German Peasants' War: A History in
Documents* (Atlantic Highlands, N.J.: Humanities Press International, 1991), 65–72.

3. When someone is executed [for theft] the lords take the stolen property as well as that [of the thief]. . . .

6. Concerning heriots,[1] where a married person dies, and claims are made upon the deceased by virtue of serfdom: Although marriage is ordained by divine and Christian ordinances to be free, . . . [if a male dies and is later charged with being a serf,] then the officials take the best head of cattle. . . .

13. We are forced to perform military service and to campaign with foreign lords and territories. . . .

14. The domain forest and other woods have been removed from our use, contrary to ancient tradition.

15. Our rulers, their officials and servants ride over the fields, hawking, beating, and hunting without any restraint, and at inconvenient times, and damage and devastate the crops.

16. The lords have taken the water that runs through our holdings, contrary to ancient tradition, and leased it to fishermen. . . .

19. The lords claim the inheritance from illegitimate children, to the exclusion of the next of kin, even if they were born free persons. . . .

23. We do not know the origin of rents and interest payments. . . .

24. We are burdened with numerous labor services. . . .

41. Game should be free [for all to hunt]. . . .

50. We are forbidden to buy and sell salt, etc., contrary to all ancient traditions. . . .

59. Concerning serfdom: We are by right born free and it is no fault of ours or of our forefathers that we have been subjected to serfdom, yet our lords wish to have and keep us as their own property, and consider that we should perform everything that they ask . . . and it may in time come to pass that they will also sell us. It is our plea that you adjudge that we should be released from serfdom, and no one else be forced into it, in which case we will perform for our lords what we are obliged to perform of old, except this burden.

---

[1] This feudal obligation required a dead peasant's family to make payment to a lord for the death of "his" serf. This "death tax" was usually paid in animals.

14

SEBASTIAN LOTZER AND CHRISTOPH SCHAPPELER

The Twelve Articles of the Upper Swabian Peasants

March 1525

From late February to early March 1525, peasant bands from three regions—the area around Baltringen, the Lake of Constance, and the Allgäu—assembled at the free imperial city of Memmingen in a rudimentary peasant parliament. They drew up lists of grievances and demands for reform. A journeyman furrier and lay preacher in the city, Sebastian Lotzer, reduced these lists to twelve basic articles. A Memmingen preacher, Christoph Schappeler, who was active in the evangelical movement and who sympathized with the peasants, provided biblical citations to prove that the Word of God supported and justified the peasants' articles. Schappeler himself was strongly influenced by Huldrych Zwingli and participated in the 1523 debate in Zurich at which Zwingli defended his Sixty-Seven Articles (Document 10). The Twelve Articles *became the most widely influential program of the Peasants' War. Peasants in virtually every area where the rebellion took place used or modified it as the basis of their demands. In this sense,* The Twelve Articles *constituted the key manifesto of the entire Peasants' War.*

The Just and Fundamental Articles of All the Peasantry and Tenants of Spiritual and Temporal Powers, Who They Think Are Oppressing Them

To the Christian reader, the peace and grace of God through Jesus Christ.

Because the peasants are assembled, there are many anti-Christians who now find reason to disparage the gospel, saying, "These are the fruits of the new gospel: to be obedient to no one, to rise up and rebel everywhere, to form military units of great violence, to band together to reform spiritual and temporal *The anti-Christians*

The fruits of the new gospel

Günther Franz, ed., Michael G. Baylor, trans., *Quellen zur Geschichte des Bauernkriegs* (Darmstadt: Wissenschaftliche Buchgesellschaft, 1963), 174–79.

authorities, to expel them, perhaps even to kill them." The following articles reply to all these godless, criminal critics, first, to stop them from disparaging the Word of God, and second, to justify on Christian grounds the disobedience, indeed the rebellion, of all the peasants. *The Articles' justification, Rom. 1*

First, the gospel is not a cause of rebellions or insurrections, because it speaks of Christ the promised Messiah, whose words and life teach nothing but love, peace, patience, and unity, so that all who believe in Christ become loving, peaceful, patient, and united. If the basis of all the peasants' articles (as will be clearly seen) is directed toward hearing the gospel and living according to it, how can the anti-Christians call the gospel a cause of the rebellion and disobedience? Although certain anti-Christians and enemies of the gospel oppose such demands and want to flare up and revolt against them, the gospel is not the cause of this but the behavior in his followers through lack of faith, so that the Word of God (which teaches love, peace and unity) is suppressed and abolished.

Second, it clearly and simply follows that since, in their articles, the peasants want to be taught and live by such a gospel, they cannot be called disobedient or seditious. If God wants to hear the peasants (who are fearfully calling for the opportunity to live according to his Word), who will blame the will of God? Who will interfere with his judgment? Indeed, who will oppose his majesty? Did he not listen to the children of Israel who cried out to him, and free them from the hand of Pharaoh? Is he unable to rescue his followers today? Yes, he will rescue them — and soon! Therefore, Christian reader, zealously read the following articles and then judge them. *Rom. 11, Isa. 40, Rom. 8, Exodus 3 and 14* *Luke 18*

Here follow the articles.

Article One

First, it is our humble desire and request, and the intention and conviction of us all, that henceforth we want to have the authority and power for a whole congregation to elect and appoint its own pastor. And the power to remove him, if he acts improperly. This elected pastor should preach the holy gospel to us purely and clearly, without any human addition, doctrine and commandments. Rather, he should always proclaim the true faith to us, prompting us to petition God for his grace, so that he *1 Tim. 3, Titus 1, Acts 14* *Deut. 17, Exodus 31, Deut. 10*

instills and confirms this same true faith in us. For if his grace is
not instilled in us, we will always remain flesh and blood, which
is useless, as is clearly stated in Scripture: Only through true
faith can we come to God, and only through his mercy will we be *John 6,*
saved. Thus, such an elected leader and pastor are necessary for *Gal. 2*
us and grounded in scripture.

Article Two

Second, since a just tithe has been established in the Old *As the whole*
Testament, and fulfilled in the New, we will gladly pay the just *Epistle to*
grain tithe[1] to the full—but in the proper way. It should be *says, Ps. 109*
given to God and distributed to his people, paid to a pastor who
clearly proclaims the Word of God. We are willing that henceforth our church wardens, chosen by the congregation, collect *Gen. 14,*
and receive this tithe. From it they shall give the parson, who *Deut. 18, 12*
has been elected by the whole congregation, enough to maintain
himself and his family modestly, according to the determination
of the whole congregation. And whatever is left over should be
distributed to the poor needy people of the village, according to
their circumstances and the determination of the congregation.
What is left over after this should be retained, in case travel is *1 Tim. 5*
necessary due to a territorial emergency. So that no land tax may *Matt. 10*
be imposed on the poor, travel expenses should be derived from *1 Cor. 9*
this surplus.

Also, if due to some emergency, one or more villages have *A Christian*
sold the rights to their tithe, and this sale can be proved to the *offer*
villages, the villages should not refuse to pay the tithe owner.
Rather, we will reach an agreement with him in a proper manner according to the circumstances, and redeem the tithe rights *Luke 6*
for a reasonable amount and in a reasonable time. But if any- *Matt. 5*
one has not bought tithe rights personally from a village, and
has received them from his forefathers, who bequeathed them *One should*
to him, we shall not be, should not be, and are not obligated to *not take*
pay him anything more—only what is needed to maintain our *anything*
from
elected pastor, to change the pastor if events warrant, and to dis- *another*
tribute alms to the needy, according to scripture. This shall be
the case regardless of whether the owners of rights to the tithe

---

[1] The *korn zehat*, sometimes also called the "major tithe" and paid on the yield of
grain and other products of the land.

are spiritual or temporal lords. We will not pay the "small tithe" at all.[2] Since the lord God created cattle freely for mankind, *Gen. 1* we regard it as an improper tithe which has been contrived by people. Thus, we will no longer pay it.

Article Three

Third, until now it has been the custom for us to be regarded *Isaiah 53* as a lord's personal property.[3] This is deplorable since Christ *1 Pet. 1* redeemed us all with the shedding of his precious blood—the *1 Cor. 7* *Rom. 13* shepherd as well as the most highly placed, without exception. *Eccles. 6* *1 Pet. 2* Thus, Scripture establishes that we are and want to be free. Not *Deut. 6* *Matt. 4* that we want to be completely free, wanting to have no authority *Luke 4* over us. God does not teach us this. We should live according *Luke 6* to his commandments, not free carnal whim. Rather, we want to love God, recognize him in our neighbor as our Lord, and we want to do everything gladly that God commanded us to do at the Last Supper. Although we should live according to his com- *Matt. 7,* mandments, they do not teach and show us that we should not *John 13* be obedient to authority. And not only to authority; rather we *Rom. 13* should humble ourselves before everyone. They also show us *Acts 5* that we should be willingly obedient to our elected and estab- lished authorities (if established for us by God) in everything that is proper and Christian. Without a doubt, as true and just *A Christian* Christians, you will also gladly release us from serfdom, or show *offer* us from the gospel that we should be serfs.[4]

Article Four

Fourth, until now it has been the custom that no poor man has *Gen. 1* had the authority to hunt game or fowl or to catch fish in flowing *Acts 10* *1 Tim. 4* water. We think that this is completely improper and unbroth- *1 Cor. 10* erly; rather, it is selfish and not compatible with the Word of *Coloss. 2* God. The authorities in some places also maintain game [for *A Christian* *offer* their own hunting], to our distress and great detriment. And we must tolerate it that unreasoning animals uselessly consume our

---

[2] The small or lesser tithe was paid on animals, especially cattle.
[3] *Aigen leüt*; lit. one's "own people"—i.e., as serfs or bondsmen.
[4] Something that the author of the work plainly thought was impossible.

crops (which God has let grow for the benefit of people). And we have to keep silent about this, which is contrary to God's will and the needs of one's neighbors. When the Lord God created man, he gave him dominion over all animals, birds in the air, and fish in the water. Thus it is our wish that, if someone owns a body of water, and he can adequately prove it in writing that the water was knowingly sold to him, it is not to be taken from him with force. Rather, for the sake of brotherly love, we must have a Christian investigation of the matter. But if someone cannot produce adequate proof of his ownership, he should inform the community of this in the proper manner. *A Christian offer*

Article Five

Fifth, we also have grievances concerning the use of woodlands. For our lordships alone have appropriated all the woods, and when the poor man needs wood, he must buy it at double the price. It is our conviction that, regardless of the kind of woods involved—whether possessed by spiritual or temporal authorities who have not bought it—it should revert to the whole community. And in the appropriate way, a community should be free to permit anyone having need to take wood home for burning without paying for it, or to take it for needed building without paying. But this must be done with the knowledge of those elected by the community to supervise such matters. If, however, the only woodland available is that which has been legally purchased, agreement should be reached with the owner in a brotherly and Christian way. But if originally the property was simply individually appropriated by someone, and then sold [to a third party], an agreement should be reached according to the circumstances of the case and our knowledge of brotherly love and holy scripture. *As shown above, in the first chapter of Gen.* *Officials should see that this does not lead to denuding the woods*

Article Six

Sixth, we have a serious grievance concerning labor services, which increase from day to day. We want to be granted a fair investigation of them, and accordingly not be so severely burdened. Rather, we should be allowed to serve graciously, as our forefathers served, according to the Word of God alone. *A Christian offer* *Rom. 10*

Article Seven

Seventh, henceforth we no longer want to let lords oppress us. Rather, if a lordship has been bestowed on someone in the correct way, he should receive his lordship through an agreement between lord and peasants. Lords should not force or compel *Luke 3,* their peasants, seeking to get more services or other dues from *1 Thess. 4* them without payment. The peasant should be able to use and enjoy his property in peace, without being burdened. But if the lord is truly in need of services, the peasant should willingly and obediently be at his disposal, but at an hour and season that are not to the peasant's detriment, and the peasant should be properly paid for his services.

Article Eight

Eighth, we are oppressed, especially those that hold their own land, because these lands cannot sustain the [rent] payments on them, and because these peasants must then forfeit their land and are ruined. [We demand] that lords let honorable people inspect these pieces of property and establish a rent that is equitable, so that the peasant does not work for nothing. For every *Matt. 10* laborer is worth his wage.

Article Nine

Ninth, we are oppressed by the way serious crimes are punished, *Isaiah 10* for new laws are constantly being made, so that we are punished *Ephes. 6* not according to the facts of a case, but sometimes out of envy *Luke 3* and sometimes out of great favoritism. It is our conviction that *Jer. 26* we should be punished according to ancient written law and the circumstances of the case, and not on the basis of favoritism.

Article Ten

Tenth, we are oppressed that some people have appropriated *As above,* meadowland as well as fields which belong to the community. We *Luke 6* will take these properties into our common hands again, unless they have in fact been legally bought. But if someone has bought *A Christian* them unfairly, the parties involved should reach a benevolent *offer* and brotherly agreement, according to the facts of the case.

Article Eleven

Eleventh, we want the custom termed heriot [or death tax] to be completely and totally abolished. For we will never tolerate or accept that the property of widows and orphans should be taken so shamelessly from them, contrary to God and honor, and that they should be robbed, as has occurred in many places (and in many forms). Those who should protect and defend us have skinned and sheared us. If they had even a slight pretext, they would have taken everything. God will no longer tolerate this, and the custom must be done away with. Henceforth no one should be obligated to pay the heriot, whether the amount is much or little.

Deut. 18
Matt. 8
Matt. 23
Isaiah 11

In Conclusion

Twelfth, it is our conclusion and final conviction that if one or more of the articles we have composed here is not in accordance with the Word of God, we will retract these articles, if they can be shown to be improper according to the Word of God. We will renounce them if they are explained to be false on the basis of Scripture. If some articles are now granted to us, and later it turns out that an injustice has been done, from that moment on these articles will be null and void, no longer in force. By the same token, if by the truth of Scripture we find other articles that are against God and a burden on our neighbors, we will declare them to be incorporated in our list. We bid God the Lord to grant it to us to live and practice every Christian teaching, for he alone and no one else is capable of giving this to us. May the peace of Christ be with us all.

Because all the articles are contained in God's Word

A Christian offer

15

THOMAS MÜNTZER[?] AND BALTHASAR HUBMAIER

The Constitutional Draft

1525

In a confession he made shortly before his execution, Thomas Müntzer said that at the end of 1524 he traveled to southwestern Germany, preached to the peasants there, and proposed articles on how to govern according to the gospel. These articles have never been firmly identified. However, it is possible that they are among a series of articles that Habsburg authorities found among the papers of Balthasar Hubmaier, an evangelical preacher at Waldshut who supported the peasants. The articles, which are known as "The Constitutional Draft," may have resulted from a collaboration between Müntzer and Hubmaier in framing basic principles for the transfer of political power from the existing rulers to the common people. The Habsburg official Johann Fabri published them in 1528 to justify Hubmaier's execution, and his version is the only known copy.

"The Constitutional Draft" urged the peasants to form a regional Christian political association so that they might live according to the gospel. The association was to invite the rulers of the region to join. If the rulers refused, the association's popular assembly had the right to elect new rulers to replace the old, and to recall rulers who acted against the common interests of the people.

---

1. . . . The people of each territory (*Landschaft*) should come together and make a union (*Bund*). The time is at hand when God will no longer tolerate the worldly lords' fleecing and flaying, fettering and stocking, forcing and driving, and other tyrannies. They do to the poor people what Herod did to the innocent little children. Thus, the murdering duke of Lorraine has given a first taste of his princely illustriousness at Saverne in Alsace and elsewhere. In order to stop this kind of thing,

---

Gunther Franz, ed., Michael G. Baylor, trans., *Quellen zur Geschichte des Bauernkriegs* (Darmstadt: Wissenschaftliche Buchgesellschaft, 1963), 231–33.

people must come together and establish a political order
according to the Word of God.

2.   Accordingly, the commons should write to its authorities once,
twice, and a third time that they should join its brotherhood
and union. If they will not join, then a territory is permitted to
take the sword from the authorities and to give it to another. If
the territory does not do this, it is complicit in the vices of the
rulers.

3.   And he [Hubmaier] taught how to appoint kings, princes,
dukes, and territorial lords. Namely, when the people have
gathered together, they should swear to keep God's Word. And
from twelve men put forward by the peasants, one should be
chosen, with no special regard given to the nobility. And should
the person chosen thereafter prove unsuitable, he may be
deposed after the region has warned him three times. And the
region should bind its members to do this by pledging together
to stake and to shed their body, honor, goods, and blood on it.

4.   But should the deposed lords seek revenge, he taught in the
fourth article, the new lord should declare them to be under
the worldly ban,[1] and if the ban has no effect, the new territorial lord shall levy troops from his land or hire soldiers at the
territory's expense, and attack the obstinate lord, until the
bloodthirsty tyrants are extirpated.

---

[1] The meaning of this secular or worldly ban is set forth in detail in Document 18, *The
Document of Articles*. The mention of this ban in "The Constitutional Draft" is one indica-
tion of its composition prior to Document 18 and early in the Peasants' War.

16

Title Page of "The Memmingen Federal Ordinance"

March 7, 1525

When the peasant bands gathered together at the free imperial city of Memmingen in early March 1525, they produced more than The Twelve Articles *(Document 14). On March 7, they agreed to a Federal Ordinance (Bundesordnung), a rudimentary constitution apparently modeled, at least in part, on the principles of "The Constitutional Draft" (Document 15). The image on the title page of this edition of "The Memmingen Federal Ordinance" (Document 17) depicts a band of armed peasants. It shows something of the variety of the commoners' preparations for battle: Some wear armor, others do not; some carry agricultural implements such as flails and billhooks as weapons, others conventional weapons such as spears and halberds. The full title of the work is "The Actions, Articles and Instructions That All the Platoons and Bands of the Peasants Have Obligated Themselves to Carry Out. 1525."*

Günther Vogler, Adolf Laube, and Max Steinmetz, *Illustrierte Geschichte der deutschen frühbürgerlichen Revolution* (Berlin: Dietz, 1974), 234.

Handlung / Artickel / vnnd Instruction / so fürgenömen worden sein vonn allen Rottenn vnnd hauffen der Pauren / so sich zesamen verpflicht haben: M:D:xxv:

17

The Memmingen Federal Ordinance

March 7, 1525

A key example of the ability of the peasants to organize themselves both militarily and politically, The Memmingen Federal Ordinance *set forth the basic conditions for membership in and the aims of a new territorial association, a Christian union or federation* (Bund). *This union was designed to both protect the commoners and be the political vehicle for the realization of their demands, which were articulated in* The Twelve Articles *(Document 14). An important provision of the document was its request that lords not provision their castles or garrison them with opponents of the rebellion. The peasants wanted to live according to divine law as expressed in the Bible, and at the document's conclusion they listed a number of evangelical clerics associated with the Reformation, whom they felt to be qualified to determine the content of divine law. Some they knew by name, others only by the position or title they held. The prominent clerics they appealed to as competent to comment on the meaning of godly law all rejected their request.*

This Christian union and association has been founded in order to praise and honor eternal, almighty God, and also by appealing to the holy gospel and the divine word to contribute to justice and divine law. It has not been founded to show contempt toward anyone or to deprive him of his rights, be he a spiritual or a secular lord. And it has been founded especially to increase brotherly love.

1. First, the honorable territorial community [*Landschaft*] of this Christian association insists that the spiritual and temporal authorities are responsible for acting according to divine law, and for not violating this law in any way, but obediently maintaining it.

2. Again, it is the honorable territorial community's will and conviction that the common peace should be maintained and that

---

Michael G. Baylor, ed. and trans., *The Radical Reformation* (Cambridge: Cambridge University Press, 1991), 239–42.

no one should violate the rights of another. But if it should occur that someone causes another to take to arms and rebel, others should not in any way assemble and form factions. And the nearest person, regardless of his social standing, should have the authority to make peace among them and to request that from now on one bid the other to make peace and restrain themselves. And if this peace that has been requested is not maintained, the one responsible for violating it should be punished accordingly.

3. Again, all [feudal] dues which are generally acknowledged, or for which there are documents with seals or a trustworthy record, however dilapidated, should be paid. But if someone thinks he can convince a person [who disputes an obligation], he should take the matter to court, but each at his own expense, and for the sake of the common territory of this association. And this concerns debts as well as tithes; other rents and payments should be suspended pending the outcome of the lawsuits.

4. Again, since castles are not part of this form of territorial [agreement], and since they are not joined in this Christian association, the residents of castles should be requested with a friendly admonition to see to it that they do not store up provisions beyond what they reasonably need for their own use. And they should not garrison these castles with persons or weapons that do not belong to this association. But if henceforth they want to garrison them, they should do this with people who are members of this association, and at their [i.e., the castle owners'] own expense and risk. The same is true of cloisters.

5. Again, if there are servants who are serving princes and lords, they should renounce their oaths, and publicly say that they have done so; and if they do this, they should be accepted into this association. Those who do not want to do this, however, should take their wives and children and leave the territory willingly. But if a lord demands [the appearance] of an official or someone else who is in this association, he should not go alone, but he should take two or three with him, and let them hear what is to be done with him, etc.

6. Again, pastors and vicars should be requested in a friendly way to preach [only] the holy gospel. And the ones who want to do this should be given what is needed to live in moderation. But those who do not want to do this should be discharged, and these pastors should be replaced with others, etc.

7. Again, if anyone wants to make an agreement with the authorities, he should not conclude it without the prior knowledge and approval of the common territorial community of this association. And if an agreement is concluded with the approval of this said territory, nonetheless the person making it should still agree to remain in this eternal covenant and Christian association.

8. Again, a captain and four cavalrymen should be designated and dispatched from each military unit of this association. They, together with the other captains and cavalry, should have the authority to negotiate suitably, so that the community does not always have to assemble.

9. No plundered property, if it has been wrongfully expropriated, should be maintained or employed, etc.

10. The craftsmen who want to take their work out of the territory should not oppose this Christian association to get the praise of their ecclesiastical superiors. Rather, if they hear that opposition to this territory is arising, they should inform this association and, if it is necessary, be ready to return right away and help save it. Soldiers should also be bound to do the same.

11. Courts should proceed and laws should be applied as has been the case previously.

12. Again, inappropriate games, blasphemy and drinking are forbidden [in this union]. Whoever does not keep this article, shall be punished according to [the degree of] his guilt.

The following theologians have been designated [as competent] to determine the substance of divine law.

Doctor Martin Luther
Philip Melanchthon
Doctor Jacob Strauss at Eisleben
Osiander at Nuremberg
Billican at Nördlingen
Matthew Zell and his associates at Strassburg
Conrad [Sam], the preacher at Ulm
[Johannes Brenz,] the preacher at Schwäbisch Hall
[Michael Keller,] the Franciscan preacher at Augsburg
[Hans Zwick,] the preacher at Riedlingen
[Sigmund Rötlin,] the preacher in the cloister at Lindau
Ulrich Zwingli and his associates at Zurich
[Matthew Alber,] the preacher at Reutlingen
[Matthew Waibel,] the preacher on the mountain at Kempten

18

The Document of Articles
May 8, 1525

The rebellious peasants composed the so-called "Document of Articles" (Artikelbrief), which linked "The Constitutional Draft" and "The Memmingen Federal Ordinance" (Documents 15 and 17). Despite its name, it was not really a listing of the articles to which the peasants subscribed; these were set out in "The Memmingen Federal Ordinance." Rather, "The Document of Articles" presupposed the existence of a federation or association such as that described in "The Memmingen Federal Ordinance," that is, a Christian union, and it spelled out the consequences that any person or institution would suffer for failing to join such a Christian union. Especially, "The Document of Articles" made explicit the meaning of the "worldly ban," which was introduced without further specification in "The Constitutional Draft." This worldly ban, modeled on the ecclesiastical ban of excommunication, amounted to a kind of total boycott or absolute shunning of the affected person or institution.

In the version of "The Document of Articles" presented here, the peasant band of the Black Forest wrote to the city of Villingen on May 8, 1525, demanding its entry into the band's Christian union and, as an ultimatum, setting forth the consequences if the city refused. The peasants also announced that they were immediately placing all castles and cloisters under the worldly ban. This was a more radical step than "The Memmingen Federal Ordinance," which merely requested that lords not use their castles as bases of opposition to the peasants.

We extend to you, the mayor, council and whole community of the city of Villingen,[1] peace and the grace of God almighty. And we admonish you to decide whether you, too, want to help divine justice and the holy gospel of our lord, Jesus Christ, and join our Christian brotherhood according to the terms of the articles which we are herewith sending you.

---

[1] A small city in the territory of Freiburg im Breisgau.

Michael G. Baylor, ed. and trans., *The Radical Reformation* (Cambridge: Cambridge University Press, 1991), 243–45.

Accordingly, we request a written answer for our messenger without delay. Dated at Verembach on the Monday after the Feast of the Holy Cross [May 8,] 1525.

The captains and council of the peasant army in the Black Forest.

The Letter of Articles

Honorable, wise and favorable lords, friends and dear neighbors. In the recent past heavy burdens, much against God and all justice, have been imposed on the poor common man in the cities and in the countryside by spiritual and worldly lords and authorities. But these [impositions] have not touched these lords in the slightest way. The result is that these burdens and grievances can no longer be borne or tolerated, unless the common man is willing to condemn himself and his progeny to a life of begging.

Accordingly, it is the proposal and intention of this Christian association, with the help of God, to make itself independent, and to do this, so far as possible, without taking up arms and without bloodshed. This can only occur if there is brotherly admonition and agreement on all relevant matters which concern the common Christian good, as encompassed in the accompanying articles.

It is our friendly request, expectation and brotherly petition that you join us willingly, and submit as friends to this Christian association and brotherhood, so that the common Christian good and brotherly love are again established and increased. If you do this, the will of God will be realized in what you do, as you fulfill his commandment about brotherly love.

But if you reject this [petition]—which we in no way foresee—we will place you under the worldly ban. And in doing so, we will regard you as under the power of the ban, as set forth in this document, until the time that you repudiate your intentions and submit willingly to this Christian association. We do not want to keep this from you, who are our dear lords, friends, and neighbors of good reputation. We request a written answer, sent with this messenger, from the council and community [of Villingen]. We commend you to God.

The Worldly Ban Is Valid in This Sense

All who are in this Christian association, on their honor and as their highest duty, will treat in the following way those who reject and refuse to enter the brotherly association and to further the common Christian good: they will have absolutely nothing to do with them, and this means that they will neither eat, drink, bathe, grind grain, bake, work the fields, nor harvest with them. Nor will they provide them, or allow anyone else to provide them, with food, grain, drink, wood, meat, salt, or anything else. They will neither buy anything from them, nor sell them anything. Rather, they will let them abide as severed, dead members in [our] affairs, as those who do not wish to promote but instead seek to hinder the Christian commonwealth and the peace of the territory.

They will also be deprived of all markets, woods, meadows, pastures, and water which are not directly in their legal power and at their disposal.[2]

And if anyone, having entered the association, then disregards it, he will also be excluded immediately and punished with the same ban. And he will be sent with wife and children to our adversaries or enemies.

Concerning Castles, Cloisters, and Ecclesiastical Foundations

Because all treachery, coercion, and corruption arise and spread from castles, cloisters, and ecclesiastical foundations, they are placed under the ban from this moment on.

But if the nobles, monks, or parsons of such castles, cloisters, or foundations want to leave them, and live in normal houses like other pious people,[3] and to join this Christian association, they and their goods and property will be accepted in a friendly manner. And if they join, they will be permitted to keep, truly and honorably and without any deprivation, everything that has been conveyed to them according to divine law.

Concerning Those Who Provision, Promote and Support the Enemies of this Christian Association

Likewise, all those who provision, promote, and support the enemies of this Christian association will be bidden in a friendly way to desist from these practices. But if they do not do this, they will also be declared to be under the worldly ban and without any property.

---

[2] *in ihren zwingen und bännen*; i.e., areas in which a feudal lord had the right of lower justice and exercised the power to make binding or compulsory decisions.

[3] The text has *frembd lüt*, but *frembd*, "foreign," is evidently an error for *fromm*, "pious."

19

The Field Ordinances of the Franconian Peasantry

April 24–27, 1525

One of the armed peasant bands in Franconia, the Bright Band, adopted the following field ordinances on April 24–27, 1525. The ordinances, as reported by Lorenz Fries, historian to the bishop of Würzburg, reveal that leadership in the army was based on a rudimentary democracy; the band as a whole, usually convened in a circle or "ring," elected its commander and other officers. The ordinances also show the peasants' concerns for religious and moral values as well as proper discipline and order. Peasant armies commonly drew on the military experience of members who had served as mercenary infantrymen and who were able to assist them in developing an efficient organization. However, when castles and monasteries were captured, rebellious peasants also engaged in destructive behavior, burning archives and libraries, looting storehouses and wine cellars, and otherwise putting the strongholds of their enemies to the sack. Such behavior was common in sixteenth-century military operations, despite the restraint enjoined by ordinances such as the following.

This ordinance is established for the honor and praise of Almighty God and for the benefit of the entire common band of the assembled peasantry.

1. First, it has been considered and regarded as necessary and right that for the proper formation of this Christian, fraternal alliance, the Word of God, which is food for the soul, should be preached and proclaimed purely and clearly to the people daily, as often as opportunity allows. . . .

2. It shall be commanded that in the bright band all blasphemy and cursing be avoided.

3. In this worthy Christian brotherhood all toasting and other disorderly and superfluous eating and drinking shall be forbidden.

4. No one shall gamble.

Tom Scott and Bob Scribner, eds. and trans., *The German Peasants' War: A History in Documents* (Atlantic Highlands, N.J.: Humanities Press International, 1991), 160–63.

5. Unchaste women are not to be tolerated in the camp.

6. The supreme commander is to be elected by the common bright band, to exercise power over all the people. Each person is to be subject and obedient to him, but with the proviso that the same supreme commander shall not undertake or negotiate anything personally without the will and knowledge of the appointed captains and councillors who have been appointed by the entire band.

7. The same supreme commander shall accept or open no letter, whether it comes from princes, lords, or others, nor send any letter or other business out of his own initiative, unless with the knowledge of the appointed captains and councillors, where these are present. If not all of them are present, he shall open or send out no letter unless three or four of the captains and councilors are present.

8. It may happen that in the course of events the supreme commander cannot on occasion deal with all the business; therefore it is necessary, and considered good that someone should be appointed alongside him, called the lieutenant, who shall be appointed by the common band and take orders from the supreme commander.

9. And to support both such superior officers against the wanton and the rebellious, it is considered that the supreme commander shall have four aides appointed alongside him, and the lieutenant two, to serve alongside them day and night, and loyally to follow their requests and orders. . . .

11. The supreme commander and the lieutenant shall have their lodgings and tents near the cannon, so that they can be found by day or night in case of need.

12. The common band reserves the right to appoint and dismiss such officers.

13. A captain is to be elected by each troop, to whom those in the troop may reveal their needs and grievances. Afterwards, the same captains shall present these grievances to the supreme commander in the presence of the appointed captains and councillors, which will be discussed by them, and so all disorder and trouble will be kept in check.

14. From each company comprising around five hundred men, one man shall be elected as color-sergeant. And the elected

color-sergeant shall be obliged, as is fitting, to exercise his office truly and honorably, as far as his honor and bodily power permit. . . .

15. A judge [*Schultheiss*] is to be appointed by the common assembly, and he is to administer justice each day, as often as the need arises, alongside the appointed assessors or jurors who have been or may in future be appointed, and to punish the evil and advance and protect justice. And in this he shall let himself be influenced by no bribes, fees, friendships, or enmities, but keep before his eyes . . . only God and his justice. The judge shall have two aides appointed to assist him.

16. One man is to be appointed by the common band as provost-marshal. He shall exercise his office in the following manner. First, whenever camp is pitched, he shall immediately erect a gallows for the punishment of the wicked and the support of pious Christian people. He shall arrest all evildoers and transgressors and hold them in secure custody, and afterwards present the misdeeds of each to the captains and councillors. Whatever orders are sent to the provost-marshal after the presentation and assessment of the accused, he is to implement. The provost-marshal shall have no power of his own to do violence to or to levy anyone, be they clerical or lay, Christian or Jew, but only on the orders, and by the will and knowledge of the supreme commander and the appointed councillors. He shall on his oath hand over the confiscated or acquired goods or money to the captains and councillors, or whoever else has so entrusted him, and not retain them in his power.

17. The provost-marshal shall also, as soon as camp is pitched, assess all the provisions brought into the camp according to fair prices, whether it be bread, wine, meat, or other victuals. . . . If corn, wheat, or oats are brought in, he shall also price them fairly and shall take a shilling from each wagon and three pence from a cart as his fee. . . .

18. For the office of master of artillery, armorer, and master of the arsenal, the common band shall appoint as commander of artillery someone who shall be in sole command of the cannon and keep it in good order and security. . . .

19. A wagon-master is to be appointed, and his command is that when camp is struck and moves off, no more wagons are to

move off and proceed than he orders. However he orders them to proceed, they shall keep that order, and the carts are not [to] be mixed in among the wagons. . . .

21. The office of master of the watch shall have four [persons] appointed to it, who are to use their true diligence so that when camp is pitched, watch will be kept as necessary.

22. Four sergeants shall be appointed by the bright band to make a battle-order. . . .

23. Then there shall be appointed a sergeant for each troop, to march alongside the ranks, and whoever shall fall out of the ranks he shall drive back into them. On the march everyone is to remain where he has been ordered and not leave the ranks, on pain of punishment.

24. Two quartermasters are to be elected to supervise the kitchens and cellars, so that they can be kept in good and uniform order. . . .

27. A master of the spoils is to be appointed in each company, so that booty will be distributed equally and no one receive more or less advantage than another. . . .

29. A paymaster shall be appointed and everyone shall pay him for provisions consumed and the like. . . .

31. Further, it has been decided that all those who join as a group and unite with this Christian assembly and brotherhood may not separate themselves from it and depart without the knowledge of the supreme commander and the councillors.

32. Henceforth, when we are encamped before a town or market, no one shall go to or enter the said town or market without the knowledge and command of the captains and councillors.

33. Also no one is to tolerate in the band any stranger who is not sworn into this brotherhood.

34. Item, in this brotherhood and union all women, maidens, widows, and orphans, young children, the old and the invalid, the sick, and women in childbirth shall be protected, defended, left unharmed and free, and shall so remain. Likewise, all millers shall be protected and left unharmed and no plough shall be stolen, but preserved for the common good. No one shall undertake by force or criminal act to attack or to harm any convent, church, chapter, or like ecclesiastical property without

the command and order of the supreme commander and the councillors.

35. Single or particular persons shall not be accepted up into this, our fraternal and Christian venture and order, where they have any dispute, disagreement, or contested matter with towns or markets or others. . . . But each person comprised in the brotherhood shall not be denied justice where he has something to say to another, especially what has occurred before this time, whatever it might have been.

36. Whatever nobleman desires to join this Christian brotherhood shall and must accept that his castle and fortifications be broken up, or shall have the power to do it himself at a suitable time. But whatever movable property he has, he shall have power to retain in his own custody. The cannon that he has in the castle should be turned over to the bright band; likewise refugee property, such as that belonging to the clergy, monks, nuns, priests, or other nobles shall be handed over to this assembly, on pain of loss of life and property. He shall henceforth keep no armored horse while this business remains unresolved. By the obligation which he has undertaken to the assembly he shall prove that he has given no support or aid in word or deed against the assembly, and will not henceforth do so, through himself or his people, whether openly or secretly.

37. Everyone shall henceforth give and receive common law, just as other citizens or peasants in towns and markets have hitherto done, and shall be subject to and remain within its jurisdiction. In the meantime, and until a reformation has been established, none of you shall demand rents, annuities, interest, entry-fines, or similar burdens, but desist until the establishment of the reformation.

38. Whoever cannot come to join us in person when he is summoned shall be empowered to send another resident pious, upright man in his place.

This ordinance is hereby published and proclaimed at Ochsenfurt on the Thursday after Low Sunday [27 April].

The peasants had two signets or seals, a small and a large, with which they sealed and concluded this document.

20

THOMAS MÜNTZER

Letter to the League at Allstedt

April 26 or 27, 1525

Thomas Müntzer wrote this emotionally charged letter from the free imperial city of Mühlhausen, which he helped make a center of the Peasants' War in Thuringia. At the height of the conflict, he wrote to former followers at Allstedt, especially members of the Union or League of the Elect (Bund der Auserwählten)*, which he had founded there probably in 1523. He urged them to rise up, participate in the rebellion, and spread the message of the insurrection to others. The inspirational letter expressed Müntzer's burning religious conviction that the time was right for the commoners to overturn the authority of the lords and seize power for themselves. Fear only of God and purifying suffering were essential to have a firm resolve and a true motivation. He also warned his followers not to be lured into misconceived compromises with the rulers out of a sense of mercy.*

As a greeting, [may] the pure fear of God [be with you], dear brothers.

How long are you going to sleep? How long will you fail to acknowledge the will of God because, in your view, he has forsaken you? Oh, how often have I told you how it must be—God cannot reveal himself otherwise? You must stand before him in resignation. If you do not do this, then the sacrifice of your heartfelt tribulation is in vain. Afterward, you have to start suffering again from the beginning. This I tell you—if you do not want to suffer for the sake of God's will, you will have to be the devil's martyrs. Therefore, guard yourselves; do not be so timid and negligent; do not flatter any longer the perverted fantasizers, the godless evildoers. Get going and fight the battle of the Lord! It is high time. Make sure that all your brothers do not mock the divine witness, otherwise they are all lost. All of Germany, France, and Italy is in motion. The master [God] wants to present his play, and now the evildoers are

Michael G. Baylor, ed. and trans., *Revelation and Revolution: Basic Writings of Thomas Müntzer* (Bethlehem, Pa.: Lehigh University Press, 1993), 190–92.

in for it. During Easter week, four churches belonging to religious foundations were destroyed at Fulda, the peasants in Klettgau and Hegau in the area of the Black Forest have risen, three thousand strong, and the band is getting bigger every day.[1] My only worry is that foolish people will allow themselves to be drawn into a false compromise because as yet they do not recognize the harm [the godless have caused].

Even if there are only three of you who are firm in God and who seek only his name and honor, you need not fear a hundred thousand. Now, at them, at them, at them! It is time. The evildoers are obviously as timid as dogs. Stir up the brothers, so that they arrive at peace and give witness to their [soul's] agitation. It is infinitely, infinitely necessary. At them, at them, at them! Do not be merciful, even though Esau offers you good words, Genesis 33[:4]. Pay no heed to the lamentations of the godless. They will bid you in a friendly manner [for mercy], cry, and plead like children. Do not let yourselves be merciful, as God commanded through Moses, Deuteronomy 7[:1–5]. And God has revealed the same thing to us. Stir up the villages and cities, and especially the miners with other good fellows who would be good for our cause. We must sleep no longer.

Look, as I wrote these words, I received a message from Salza informing me how the people wanted to take the official of Duke George from the castle, because he secretly wanted to kill three of them. The peasants of the Eichsfeld have taken up arms against their lords, and shortly they will show them no mercy. May events of this kind be an example for you. You must go at them, at them! The time is here! Balthasar and Barthel Krump, Valentin, and Bischof advance first to the dance![2] Pass this letter on to the miners. I have received word that my printer will come in a few days. Right now I can do nothing else. Otherwise I would give the brothers enough instruction for their hearts to become greater than all the castles and armor of the godless evildoers on earth.

At them, at them, while the fire is hot! Do not let your sword get cold, do not let your arms go lame! Strike—cling, clang!—on the anvils of Nimrod.[3] Throw their towers to the ground! As long as [the godless] live, it is not possible for you to be emptied of human fear. You cannot be told about God as long as they rule over you. At them, at them, while you have daylight! God leads you—follow, follow! The story

---

[1] In his confession, Müntzer said that in late 1524 he traveled to southwestern Germany and preached to the peasants of the Klettgau and Hegau regions.

[2] These individuals were key followers of Müntzer at Allstedt.

[3] The Old Testament figure of Nimrod was a tyrannical ruler and the builder of the tower of Babel. Here he symbolized the German territorial princes.

is already written—Matthew 24, Ezekiel 34, Daniel 74, Ezra 16, Revelation 6—scriptural passages that are all interpreted by Romans 13.

Therefore, do not let yourselves be frightened. God is with you, as it is written in 2 Chronicles 12. God says this: "You shall not be fearful. You shall not fear this great multitude, for it is not your fight, but rather that of the Lord. It is not you who fight there. Act bravely. You will see the hip of the Lord above you." When Jehoshaphat heard these words he fell down. Do likewise and through God—may he strengthen you—without fear of man and in true faith. Amen.

Dated at Mühlhausen, [April 26 or 27] in the year 1525.

THOMAS MÜNTZER, a servant of God against the godless.

21

MICHAEL GAISMAIR

Territorial Constitution for the Tirol

February or March 1526

In May 1525, the rebellious peasants of the Tirol elected Michael Gaismair, an official of the bishop of Brixen, as their leader. When the authorities suppressed the initial revolt centered around Brixen, Gaismair fled to Switzerland and began recruiting a new army from refugees there. He also came under the influence of Zwingli's Reformation in Zurich. He planned to invade the Tirol from the west, overthrow the Habsburgs, and establish a new republican government and a social order based on the civil equality of all citizens. Although there are questions about Gaismair's authorship, historians have concluded that he wrote the following constitution in February or March 1526 as a program to recruit soldiers for his army.

In addition to religious reform based on Reformation principles, Gaismair called for reforms of the legal system; financial reform of interest, customs, and tithe payments and the introduction of a new coinage; provisions for social welfare and security; proposals for economic

Michael G. Baylor, ed. and trans., *The Radical Reformation* (Cambridge: Cambridge University Press, 1991), 254–60.

*development; and reform of the key mining sector of the economy, espe-
cially its public ownership and new regulations to ensure fairness and
an end to oligopolistic advantages enjoyed by merchant-capitalist firms.
Although Gaismair's attempt to establish a new government for the Tirol
ultimately failed, the rebellion in this mountainous region lasted longer
than elsewhere. Gaismair eventually fled south into Venetian territory,
where agents of the Habsburgs assassinated him.*

---

*This Is the Territorial Constitution Which Michael Gaismair Wrote in the
Year 1526*[1]

First you will swear to bring together body and goods, not to separate
from one another, but to work and live with one another, though at all
times acting after consultation with, and being obedient to your superior
authorities.[2] And in all matters you swear not to pursue selfish interests
but rather to pursue first of all the honor of God and then the common
good, so that almighty God will be gracious and assist us (as he has
often promised all who are obedient to his commandments). We should
rely completely on God, for he is entirely truthful and deceives no one.

Second, you swear to expel all godless people, who persecute the
eternal Word of God, burden the poor commoner, and impede the common good.

Third, you swear to establish and then live completely according to
laws which are wholly Christian, and which in all matters are founded
only on the holy word of God.

Fourth, all privileges[3] should be eliminated, for they are contrary to
the word of God and falsify justice, in that no one should have an advantage over others.

Fifth, all encircling walls around cities, castles, and fortifications in
the territory should be torn down. And thereafter there should no longer be cities but only villages, so that there are no differences among
people in the sense that one is higher than another or able to do wrong
to another. For [with walls] there would be disorder in the whole territory, and pride and insurrection might arise. Rather, there should be
complete equality in the territory.

---

[1] The copyist provided the work's title.

[2] At the outset, the document takes the form of an oath sworn by recruits to Gaismair's army.

[3] *freyhaitten* (*Freiheiten*), "freedoms" or liberties, but in the sense of privileges, rights
enjoyed by some but denied to others. Hence, civil equality is an essential principle of
Gaismair's constitution.

Sixth, all images, statues, and chapels which are not in parish churches should be abolished together with the Mass in the whole territory, for they are an abomination before God and completely unchristian.

Seventh, the word of God should always be preached faithfully and truthfully in Gaismair's territory,[4] and all sophistry and legalism should be eliminated, and the books which contain them burned.[5]

Eighth, the courts throughout the territory should be arranged in the most convenient way, and the clergy excluded from them, so that they are administered with the least cost.

Ninth, the whole population of every court district should elect a judge every year and eight jurors, to exercise legal power for that year. . . .

Eleventh, a central government should be established for the territory, for which Brixen[6] would be the best location, since it has many parsonages and other facilities, and is in the centre of the territory. And the governors should be elected from all sections of the territory, as well as some from the mines.[7] . . .

Thirteenth, where the government is located [i.e., provisionally in Brixen] a university should be established where only the word of God is taught. And three learned men of this institution, who are well versed in the word of God and knowledgeable about divine Scripture (from which alone the justice of God may be expounded), should always sit in the government. They should judge and direct all matters according to the commandments of God as they pertain to a Christian people. . . .

With respect to customs payments, it appears to me in the interest of the common man that customs be entirely abolished within the territory. But on the borders customs payments should be established and maintained, so that what comes into the territory is not charged customs duty, but what leaves the territory is so charged.

With respect to the tithe, each should pay it according to the commandment of God. And it should be employed in the following manner: according to the teaching of St. Paul, there should be a pastor in each congregation who proclaims the word of God. And he should be supported in his honorable deeds from the tithe. And the remainder of the tithe should be given to the poor. But order should be maintained

---

[4] The reference to the Tirol as "Gaismair's territory" is an addition of the copyist.

[5] All works of scholastic theology and Roman law.

[6] Today, Bressanone in the Italian Tirol.

[7] Gaismair made special provision for the miners to elect representatives who would be officials of the central government because miners were not included in traditional communal forms of association.

among the poor, so that no one goes begging from house to house. This is to prevent idleness among many lazy people who are clearly able to work.

Cloisters and the buildings of the Teutonic Knights should be transformed into hospitals. In some, the sick should live together and be provided with every care and medical attention. In others, old people who are no longer able to work on account of their age should live, and poor orphans, who should be taught and raised to be honorable. But where there are poor people living in their own cottages, they should be helped according to the degree of their need from the tithe or from charity, according to the advice of each judge in his administrative district, where these people are the best known. Where the tithe is not sufficient to maintain the pastor and the poor, each person should contribute alms in good faith and according to his [or her] capacity. And where there is a deficit beyond this, the final payment should be provided [as a tax] from people's incomes.[8] . . . The poor should not only be provided with food and drink but also with clothing and other necessities.

So that good order is maintained throughout the territory in all matters, four commanders and a commander-in-chief should be established for the whole territory. And in the event of war they should be responsible for all matters pertaining to the security of the territory. . . .

The bogs, lowlands, and other unfruitful places in the territory should also be made fertile, and the common good should not be allowed to deteriorate because of some people who are selfish. All the bogs from Meran to Trent could be dried and many livestock, cows, and sheep maintained on them. Much more grain could also be cultivated in many places, so that the territory would be provided with meat. . . .

At a convenient time each year, in every district the whole community should work in the fields and the commons, clear them, and make good meadowland, thus thoroughly improving the territory. No one in the territory should practice lending,[9] so that no one is tainted by the sin of usury. [Concerning manufacturing:] So that shortages do not arise and good order is maintained, and also so that no one is overpaid or deceived, but so that fair prices and good wares are found in all matters, in the beginning one place in the territory should be designated—for which Trent would be convenient on account of its prosperity and central

---

[8] Gaismair envisioned an income tax as the fairest way to supplement the tithe and charity, should additional funds be required to carry out the government's function of caring for the needy.

[9] *Khaufmanschaft* (*Kaufmanschaft*), commerce or business, but here in the sense of lending money.

location—where all crafts are to be set up, and to which they are to be shifted from the countryside—crafts such as the making of silk cloth, caps, brass wares, velvet, shoes, and other things.[10] And a general official should be established, who has charge of all these things. And what cannot be obtained in the territory, such as spices, should be ordered from outside. [And this official should see to it that] in some convenient places in the territory shops are maintained in which many things are available. And he should see to it that a profit is never made and that only the costs which have been incurred are figured into the price. . . .

All chalices and jewelry should be taken from all churches and ecclesiastical buildings, melted down, and used for the common needs of the territory.

Good relations should also be maintained with bordering countries. The Savoyards in the territory should not be allowed to wander around [as peddlers].[11] Henceforth a market should be maintained in the region of the Etsch river and one in the valley of the Inn.[12] The whole territory should have a single set of weights and measures and a single set of laws. The borders and passes should be maintained in good condition. A considerable sum of money should be held in reserve in case the territory becomes involved in an unforeseen war. And the buildings and property of expelled nobility or others should be used to pay the expenses of the courts.

Concerning the Mines

First, all the refineries, collieries, ore, silver, copper, and what belongs to them and are found in the territory, and which are the property of the nobility and foreign merchants and their companies—such as the Fugger, Hochstetter, Baumgarter, Bumpler, and the like—should be brought into common territorial hands.[13] For they have managed them badly and have exercised their rights by demanding unjust profits, getting money by shedding human blood. They have deceived the common man and the worker with bad wares [at company stores]. . . . And they have so burdened the whole world with their unchristian usury, through

[10] It is unclear why Gaismair wanted to centralize all craft production in one location, other than ease of supervision.

[11] Traveling merchants from Savoy evidently harmed native craftspeople by undercutting their prices.

[12] These market locations were evidently determined for geographic reasons. The Etsch flows south and the Inn north, thus providing convenient transportation.

[13] Famous sixteenth-century south German merchant banking houses concentrated in the city of Augsburg.

which they accumulated their princely riches, that they should be justly punished and this situation abolished.

Accordingly, a supervising manager should be established by the territory, with responsibility for controlling all the mines and all commerce and [for rendering] an annual account. And no one [i.e., a private party] should be allowed to refine metals; rather the whole territory, through this supervising official, should license the refining of all ores, determining ore prices as fairly as possible, paying the workers in cash, and henceforth not making payment with natural products, so that in the future the rural inhabitants and the miners may live together peacefully.

This same official should maintain good order in the refineries and give the territory a considerable income from the mines. . . . For it is through mining that the territory is able to obtain the most income with the least hardship.

This is the territorial constitution that Gaismair would proclaim if he were a prince lazing beside a stove.[14]

---

[14] An ironic comment by the copyist.

4

The Debate on the Reformation and the Peasants' War

22

MARTIN LUTHER

Admonition to Peace: A Reply to the Twelve Articles
April 1525

Luther responded to The Twelve Articles *(Document 14), the peasants' most influential program, in his* Admonition to Peace: A Reply to the Twelve Articles, *which he probably completed in the second half of April 1525. In his discussion of the peasants' program, Luther separately addressed both the lords and the peasants, first condemning the princes and lords for having brought on the rebellion by suppressing the gospel and by their unjust economic demands, and then condemning the peasants for resorting to armed insurrection against those whom God had placed over them as their rulers and for using the cause of the gospel to support their demands. He blamed evil preachers for having misled the peasants—with Thomas Müntzer undoubtedly at the top of his list—and urged both sides to compromise and accept a peaceful resolution of the conflict. He also warned against the terrible consequences that could result if the effort to resolve the conflict failed.*

The peasants who have now banded together in Swabia have formulated their intolerable grievances against the rulers in twelve articles, and have undertaken to support them with certain passages of Scripture. Now

Martin Luther, *Luther's Works*, ed. Jaroslav Pelikan and Helmut T. Lehmann, trans. Charles M. Jacobs, rev. Robert C. Schultz (St. Louis: Concordia, 1955–), 46:17–43.

they have published them in printed form. The thing about them that pleases me most is that, in the twelfth article, they offer to accept instruction gladly and willingly, if there is need or necessity for it, and are willing to be corrected, to the extent that it can be done by clear, plain, undeniable passages of Scripture. And it is indeed right and proper that no one's conscience should be instructed or corrected except by Holy Scripture.

Now if that is their serious and sincere meaning . . . there is good reason to hope that things will be well. . . . But if this offer of theirs is only pretense and show (without a doubt there are some people like that among them for it is impossible for so big a crowd all to be true Christians . . .) then without a doubt [my instruction] will accomplish very little, or, in fact, it will contribute to their great injury and eternal ruin. . . .

To the Princes and Lords

We have no one on earth to thank for this disastrous rebellion, except you princes and lords, and especially you blind bishops and mad priests and monks, whose hearts are hardened, even to the present day. You do not cease to rant and rave against the holy gospel, even though you know that it is true and that you cannot refute it. In addition, as temporal rulers you do nothing but cheat and rob the people so that you may lead a life of luxury and extravagance. The poor common people cannot bear it any longer. The sword is already at your throats, but you think that you sit so firm in the saddle that no one can unhorse you. This false security and stubborn perversity will break your necks, as you will discover. . . .

For you ought to know, dear lords, that God is doing this because this raging of yours cannot, will not, and ought not be endured for long. You must become different men and yield to God's word. If you do not do this amicably and willingly, then you will be compelled to do it by force and destruction. If these peasants do not compel you, others will. . . . It is not the peasants, dear lords, who are resisting you; it is God himself, to visit your raging upon you. Some of you have said that you will stake land and people on exterminating the Lutheran teaching. What would you think if you were to turn out to be your own prophets, and your land and people were already at stake? Do not joke with God, dear lords! . . .

To make your sin still greater, and guarantee your merciless destruction, some of you are beginning to blame this affair on the gospel and say that it is the fruit of my teaching. Well, well, slander away, dear lords! . . .

If it is still possible to give you advice, my lords, give way a little to the will and wrath of God. . . . You will lose nothing by kindness; and even if you did lose something, the preservation of peace will pay you back ten times. But if there is open conflict you may lose both your property and your life. Why risk danger when you can achieve more by following a different way that is also the better way?

The peasants have just published twelve articles, some of which are so fair and just as to take away your reputation in the eyes of God and the world. . . .

In the first article they ask the right to hear the gospel and choose their pastors. You cannot reject this request with any show of right, even though this article does indeed make some selfish demands, for they allege that these pastors are to be supported by the tithes, and these do not belong to the peasants. . . .

The other articles protest economic injustices, such as the death tax. These protests are also right and just, for rulers are not appointed to exploit their subjects for their own profit and advantage, but to be concerned about the welfare of their subjects. And the people cannot tolerate it very long if their rulers set confiscatory tax rates and tax them out of their very skins. What good would it do a peasant if his field bore as many gulden as stalks of wheat if the rulers only taxed him all the more and then wasted it as though it were chaff to increase their luxury, and squandered his money on their own clothes, food, drink, and buildings? . . .

To the Peasants

So far, dear friends, you have learned only that I agree that it is unfortunately all too true that the princes and lords who forbid the preaching of the gospel and oppress the people unbearably deserve to have God pull them down from their thrones. . . . Nevertheless, you, too, must be careful that you take up your cause justly and with a good conscience. If you have a good conscience, you have the comforting advantage that God will be with you, and will help you. Even though you did not succeed for a while, or even suffered death, you would win in the end, and you would preserve your souls eternally with all the saints. But if you act unjustly and have a bad conscience, you will be defeated. And even though you might win for a while and even kill all the princes, you would suffer the eternal loss of your body and soul in the end. For you, therefore, this is no laughing matter. The eternal fate of your body and soul is involved. . . .

I will not spare you the earnest warning that I owe you, even though some of you have been so poisoned by the murderous spirits that you will hate me for it and call me a hypocrite.[1] That does not worry me; it is enough for me if I save some of the goodhearted and upright men among you from the danger of God's wrath. The rest I fear as little as they despise me much; and they shall not harm me. I know One who is greater and mightier than they are. . . .

In the first place, dear brethren, you bear the name of God and call yourselves a "Christian association" or union, and you allege that you want to live and act according to divine law. Now you know that the name, word, and titles of God are not meant to be assumed idly or in vain. . . .

Second, it is easy to prove that you are taking God's name in vain and putting it to shame; nor is there any doubt that you will, in the end, encounter all misfortune, unless God is not true. For here is God's word, spoken through the mouth of Christ, "All who take the sword shall perish by the sword" [Matt. 26:52]. That means nothing else than that no one, by his own violence, shall arrogate authority to himself; but as Paul says, "Let every person be subject to the governing authorities with fear and reverence" [Rom 13:1]. . . .

Third, you say that the rulers are wicked and intolerable, for they will not allow us to have the gospel; they oppress us too hard with the burdens they lay on our property, and they are ruining us in body and soul. I answer: The fact that the rulers are wicked and unjust does not excuse disorder and rebellion, for the punishing of wickedness is not the responsibility of everyone, but of the worldly rulers who bear the sword. . . . Now you cannot deny that your rebellion actually involves you in such a way that you make yourselves your own judges and avenge yourselves. You are quite unwilling to suffer any wrong. That is contrary not only to Christian law and the gospel, but also to natural law and equity. . . .

The rulers unjustly take your property; that is the one side. On the other hand, you take from them their authority, in which their whole property and life and being consist. Therefore you are far greater robbers than they, and you intend to do worse things than they have done. . . .

Can you not think it through, dear friends? If your enterprise were right, then any man might become judge over another. Then authority, government, law, and order would disappear from the world; there would be nothing but murder and bloodshed. . . .

---

[1] By "murderous spirits" Luther was thinking especially of Thomas Müntzer and Andreas Bodenstein of Karlstadt, radical reformers whom he elsewhere referred to as "prophets of murder."

What do you think that Christ will say about this? You bear his name, and call yourselves a "Christian association," and yet you are so far from being Christian, and your actions and lives are so horribly contrary to his law, that you are not worthy to be called heathen or Turks. You are much worse than these, because you rage and struggle against the divine and natural law, which all heathen keep.

See, dear friends, what kind of preachers you have and what they think of your souls. I fear that some prophets of murder have come among you, who would like to use you so they can become lords in the world, and they do not care that they are endangering your life, property, honor, and soul, in time and eternity.[2] If, now, you really want to keep the divine law, as you boast, then do it. There it stands! God says, "Vengeance is mine; I will repay" [Rom. 12:19], and, "Be subject not only to good lords, but also to the wicked" [1 Pet. 2:18]. If you do this, well and good; if not, you may, indeed, cause a calamity, but it will finally come upon you. . . .

And now we want to move on and speak of the law of Christ, and of the gospel, which is not binding on the heathen, as the other law is. For if you claim you are Christians and like to be called Christians and want to be known as Christians, then you must also allow your law to be held up before you rightly. Listen, then, dear Christians, to your Christian law! Your Supreme Lord, Christ, whose name you bear, says, in Matthew 6 [5:39–41], "Do not resist one who is evil. If anyone forces you to go one mile, go with him two miles. If anyone wants to take your coat, let him have your cloak too. If anyone strikes you on one cheek, offer him the other too." Do you hear this, O Christian association? How does your program stand in the light of this law? . . .

Leave the name Christian out, I say, and do not use it to cover up your impatient, disorderly, un-Christian undertaking. I shall not let you have that name, but so long as there is a heartbeat in my body, I shall do all I can, through speaking and writing, to take that name away from you. . . .

In saying this it is not my intention to justify or defend the rulers in the intolerable injustices you suffer from them. They are unjust and commit heinous wrongs against you; that I admit. If, however, neither side accepts instruction and you start to fight with each other—may God prevent it!—I hope that neither side will be called Christian. Rather I hope that God will, as is usual in these situations, use one rascal to punish the other. . . .

---

[2] Again, Luther ascribes the insurrection to the influence of radical reformers such as Müntzer.

On this basis it is now easy to reply to all your articles. Even though they all were just and equitable in terms of natural law, you have still forgotten the Christian law. You have not been putting this program into effect and achieving your goals by patiently praying to God, as Christians ought to do, but have instead undertaken to compel the rulers to give you what you wanted by using force and violence. This is against the law of the land and against natural justice. The man who composed your articles is no godly and honest man. His marginal notes refer to many chapters of Scripture on which the articles are supposed to be based.[3] But he talks with his mouth full of nothing, and leaves out the passages which would show his own wickedness and that of your cause. He has done this to deceive you, incite you, and to bring you into danger. . . .

To sum it up, everything [in your articles] is concerned with worldly and temporal affairs. You want power and wealth so that you will not suffer injustice. The gospel, however, does not become involved in the affairs of the world, but speaks of our life in the world in terms of suffering, injustice, the cross, patience, and contempt for this life and temporal wealth. How, then, does the gospel agree with you? You are only trying to give your unevangelical and un-Christian enterprise an evangelical appearance. . . .

It is true, of course, that the rulers may suppress the gospel in cities or places where the gospel is, or where there are preachers; but you can leave these cities or places and follow the gospel to some other place. It is not necessary, for the gospel's sake, for you to capture or occupy the city or place; on the contrary, let the ruler have his city; you follow the gospel. . . .

ON THE FIRST ARTICLE

"The entire community should have the power and authority to choose and appoint a pastor." This article is just only if it is understood in a Christian sense, even though the chapters indicated in the margin do not support it. If the possessions of the parish come from the rulers and not from the community, then the community cannot give these possessions to one whom they choose. . . .

ON THE SECOND ARTICLE

The pastor "shall receive out of this tithe [a modest, sufficient maintenance for him and his]; the remainder shall be distributed to the poor

---

[3] As noted in Document 14, the furrier and lay preacher Sebastian Lotzer drew up *The Twelve Articles* by summarizing the complaints of various peasant groups. The Memmingen pastor Christoph Schappeler supplied the scriptural references justifying their demands.

and needy." This article is nothing but theft and highway robbery. They want to appropriate for themselves the tithes, which are not theirs but the rulers', and want to use them to do whatever they please. Oh, no, dear friends! That is the same as deposing the rulers altogether. . . .

ON THE THIRD ARTICLE

You assert that no one is to be the serf of anyone else, because Christ has made us all free. That is making Christian freedom a completely physical matter. . . . This article, therefore, absolutely contradicts the gospel. It proposes robbery, for it suggests that every man should take his body away from his lord, even though his body is the lord's property. A slave can be a Christian, and have Christian freedom, in the same way that a prisoner or a sick man is a Christian, and yet not free. This article would make all men equal, and turn the spiritual kingdom of Christ into a worldly, external kingdom; and that is impossible. A worldly kingdom cannot exist without an inequality of persons, some being free, some imprisoned, some lords, some subjects, etc. . . .

ON THE OTHER EIGHT ARTICLES

The other articles, which discuss the freedom to hunt game animals and birds, to catch fish, to use wood from the forest, their obligation to provide free labor, the amount of their rents and taxes, the death tax, etc., are all matters for the lawyers to discuss. It is not fitting that I, an evangelist, should judge or make decisions in such matters. I am to instruct and teach men's consciences in things that concern divine and Christian matters; there are books enough about other things in the imperial laws. . . .

Admonition to Both Rulers and Peasants

Now, dear sirs, there is nothing Christian on either side and nothing Christian is at issue between you; both lords and peasants are discussing questions of justice and injustice in heathen, or worldly, terms. Furthermore, both parties are acting against God and are under his wrath, as you have heard. For God's sake, then, take my advice! Take a hold of these matters properly, with justice and not with force or violence and do not start endless bloodshed in Germany. . . .

Both Scripture and history are against you lords, for both tell how tyrants are punished. . . .

Scripture and experience are also against you peasants. They teach that rebellion has never had a good end and that God always keeps his word exactly, "He that takes the sword will perish by the sword" [Matt.

26:52]. . . . In short, God hates both tyrants and rebels; therefore he sets them against each other, so that both parties perish shamefully, and his wrath and judgment upon the godless are fulfilled. . . .

I, therefore, sincerely advise you to choose certain counts and lords from among the nobility and certain councilmen from the cities and ask them to arbitrate and settle this dispute amicably. . . .

If you do not follow this advice—God forbid!—I must let you come to blows. But I am innocent of your souls, your blood, or your property. The guilt is yours alone. . . . In any case, my conscience assures me that I have faithfully given you my Christian and fraternal advice. God grant that it helps! Amen.

23

Title Page of To the Assembly of the Common Peasantry

May 1525

The single most developed and firmly grounded justification for the great insurrection of the commoners in 1525 was the tract To the Assembly of the Common Peasantry *(Document 24), which responded to the arguments of Luther's* Admonition to Peace: A Reply to the Twelve Articles *(Document 22). The title page of this key tract conveyed a powerful symbolic message. Beneath the work's lengthy title (see Document 24 for the complete translation) is an image entitled "Now Is the Hour and Time of the Wheel of Fortune. God Knows Who Will Remain on Top." At its center, the image depicts the pope bound to a wheel of fortune that is being turned by a monk (Luther?). To the left of these central figures, a band of armed commoners, on foot, confronts a squadron of mounted clerics and nobles, who are depicted on the right side. At the top corners, the commoners are labeled "Here peasants, good Christians"; the prelates and lords are labeled "Here Romanists and Sophists." Beneath the image is the rhyming motto "Wer meret Schwyz . . . Der herren gytz" ("What increases the Swiss? The greed of the lords"). "Turning Swiss" was a shorthand expression for the ideals of personal freedom and republican liberty, which many identified with the Swiss Confederation. The lords regarded such republicanism, especially when embodied in a Christian union, as treachery and chaos.*

Herzog August Bibliothek Wolfenbüttel: 189.27 Theol. (126).

An die versamlung gemayner Pawer=
schafft/ so in Hochteütscher Nation/ vnd vil ande
rer ozt/ mit empözung vñ aufftrür entstandē. ⁊c.
ob ir empözung billicher oder vnpillicher ge
stalt geschehe/ vnd was sie der Oberkait
schuldig oder nicht schuldig seind+⁊c+
gegründet auß der heyligen Göt=
lichen geschzifft/ von Oberlen=
dischen mitbrüdern gütter
maynung außgangen
vnd beschziben. ⁊c.

Hie ist des Glückradts stund vnd zeyt
Gott wayst wer der oberist bleybt.

Hie pawrßman   Hie Romanisten
güt Christen.   vnd Sophisten.

Wer meret Schwytz   Der herzen gytz.

114

24

CHRISTOPH SCHAPPELER[?]

To the Assembly of the Common Peasantry

May 1525

---

*This important tract was published anonymously in Nuremberg in early
May 1525. Although its authorship is uncertain, historian Peter Blickle
has argued that Christoph Schappeler, the Memmingen pastor who
contributed the scriptural citations to* The Twelve Articles *(Document
14), probably wrote it.*[1] *The work presents the most thoroughly developed
and forcefully presented justification for the Peasants' War that anyone
composed at the time. In this sense, it represents the major ideological
statement of the peasants' position. It also responds directly and in detail
to Luther's arguments (in Documents 8 and 22) that rebellion is never
justified and that the peasants had no right to claim a religious foundation for their actions. The tract mentioned Luther only indirectly, and its
author began by citing points of agreement with him. But the author then
went on to refute Luther's claims by arguing that subjects have a right to
disobey, even to depose, rulers who are unjust and claim unlimited power.
The tract also developed a case for the superiority of republican over
hereditary or monarchical rule, called for a new political order modeled
on the republicanism of the Swiss Confederation, and urged the rebellious
peasants to maintain solidarity with one another.*

---

*To the assembly of the common peasantry which has come together in
revolt and insurrection in the high German nation and many other
places. Concerning whether their rebellion takes place justly or unjustly,
and what they owe or do not owe the authorities, etc., based on holy
divine Scripture. Issued and discussed with good intentions
by your brothers in upper Germany, etc.*

[1] Peter Blickle, "Republiktheorie aus revolutionärer Erfahrung (1525)," in Peter
Blickle, ed., *Verborgene republikanische Traditionen in Oberschwaben* (Tübingen: Bibliotheca Academica, 1998), 195–210.

Michael G. Baylor, ed. and trans., *The Radical Reformation* (Cambridge: Cambridge
University Press, 1991), 101–29.

Grace be with you and the eternal peace of God, from the Father and our Lord, Jesus Christ, who gave himself for our sins to save us from this present evil age according to the will of God, our Lord. May he be praised forever and ever. Amen.

Dear brothers in Christ, you know that the Lord says, "Render unto Caesar that which is Caesar's," etc. Cling to this saying in Matthew chapter 23 [rather, Mt. 22:21], just as Christ himself also gave the tax money to the emperor, Matthew 17[:24–27]. Look now, my dear brothers, the lord of heaven and earth, the true God, subjected himself to worldly authority, and voluntarily made himself liable to taxation, to give us an example to imitate. "The servant should never be above his lord." Because of this commandment, we cannot excuse ourselves from the terrible punishment, as St. Paul said to the Romans in chapter 13[:2–6], "He who resists the authorities opposes the order of God . . . and he will incur judgment. . . . For the authorities do not bear the sword in vain. They are servants of God. Therefore one should pay taxes and other dues," etc.

In this respect, dear brothers, it is a shocking sacrilege to oppose the authorities and not be obedient to them.

For as St. Paul says in this passage, "There is no authority but from God" [Rom. 13:1]. In truth, if there were no authority, the human race would perish in a shorter time than through the tortures of godless tyrants. For the hairy worm[2] would tear itself apart like a poisonous viper or a mad dog. The human race is most evilly inclined from childhood on, Genesis 6[:5] and 8[:21]. Again, Isaiah 59[:7], "Their feet run swiftly to shed blood," etc. "Their paths are those of destruction and desolation, and they do not know the path of peace."

Thus, you can see how necessary the authorities are for us, and how God ordained them because of our great need. Thus, both great need and divine commandment compel us to be obedient to authorities, "and even if they are rogues," as some translate St. Peter into German, 1 Peter 2[:18]. . . .

Chapter One. True Christian Faith Needs No Human Authority

As a basic proof of this, we have taken from divine law and Scripture three mighty and irrefutable sayings, which the gates of hell with their entire knighthood are not able to destroy. First, Matthew 7[:12], "Everything that you wish people to do to you, do the same to them," etc. Second, Matthew 22[:39, 37], "Yes, God equates brotherly love with his love

[2] That is, human nature as corrupted by original sin.

[for mankind] . . . which should come from the whole mind, the whole heart and soul." Third, St. Paul wrote to the Galatians, 3[:28], "Here is neither lord nor servant. . . . We are all one in Christ, thus indeed one," and to the Ephesians, 4[:15–16], "One shall be a limb of the other, to make one body from us all, under the head, Jesus Christ." . . .

Chapter Two. Only the Unchristian Way of Life Requires Human Authority

The carnal, unchristian, lustful life and its power rule so strongly in us and damn the Christian spirit in us so completely that from our youth on we are inclined to evil. . . . And we are so drowned in an unchristian essence that all love and fear of God, and also brotherly loyalty, are extinguished in us. . . .

The torturing punishments of hell are never so terrible that they would drive us from evil if there were no temporal fear and punishment. . . .

Chapter Three. The Obligations of a Christian Official, Be He Prince, Pope, or Emperor

. . . [E]ach authority holds office as a steward of God. Oh, would to God that such a person be worthy of the office to which God has ordained him! About which Paul says to the Ephesians [Eph. 6:9], "Consider, you lords, that your lord is also in heaven." The divine King David considered this deeply and said, "Not us, Lord; not us, Lord; it is your name that brings honor" [Ps. 115:1].

In sum, we all belong to God in body and soul. And each authority, be it spiritual or temporal, has been established only to tend God's lambs. . . .

But now it is certain that each region or city must have a common fund with which to build roads and bridges, to protect the region, and always to protect the common good, which we presently have a great need for. And what Christian would oppose this? And who would not give, out of brotherly love, the required part of his wealth in order to protect himself and to maintain his wife and children? . . .

In sum, each authority should collect taxes, customs fees, etc., in no other capacity than as a loyal, dear foster-parent, who uses his budget for the benefit of the poor and the orphans. . . . On these grounds and no other, we are obliged to pay taxes, customs, etc., and certainly not, as the scribes and lawyers jabber, because of their own ancient laws or rights. . . .

In truth, offices, whether of prince or lord, are an unbearably heavy burden from which a true Christian derives little joy, and which he endures with a quaking heart, in constant worry about how he can justify his office. Therefore, every official, be he of high or low estate, should rightly bid almighty God with a Christian spirit and fervent heart to grant him wisdom and understanding through divine grace, so that he can perform his office completely and properly, and can give an accounting of it before God and the world. . . .

Chapter Four. On False and Unlimited Power, Which One Is Not Obliged to Obey

All the popes, emperors, kings, etc. who puff themselves up in their own estimation above other pious poor Christians, claiming to be a better kind of human—as if their lordship and authority to rule others were innate—do not want to recognize that they are God's stewards and officials. And they do not govern according to his commandment to maintain the common good and brotherly unity among us. . . .

Therefore, whichever prince or lord invents and sets up his own self-serving burdens and commands, rules falsely, and he dares impudently to deceive God, his own lord. Where are you, you werewolves, you band of Behemoths,[3] with your financial tricks which impose one burden after another on the poor people? This year a labor service is voluntary, next year it becomes compulsory. In most cases this is how your old customary law has grown. . . . May God, in his justice, not tolerate the terrible Babylonian captivity in which we poor people are driven to mow the lords' meadows, to make hay, to cultivate the fields, to sow flax in them, to cut it, comb it, heat it, wash it, pound it, and spin it—yes, even to sew their underpants on their arses. We also have to pick peas and harvest carrots and asparagus.

Help us, God! Where has such misery ever been heard of! They tax and tear out the marrow of the poor people's bones, and we have to pay interest on that! Where are they, with their hired murderers and horsemen, the gamblers and whoremasters, who are stuffed fuller than puking dogs? . . .

And nevertheless, no one can turn up his nose at them, or he is immediately treated like a treacherous rogue—put in the stocks, beheaded, quartered! He is shown less pity than a mad dog.

---

[3] A term the author uses repeatedly to refer to the princes and lords; cf. Job 40:15–24.

Did God give them such power? On the peak of what monk's cowl is it written?[4] . . .

The basic cause and source of the whole confederation of the Swiss was the unlimited, tyrannical power of the nobility and other authorities. For daily, with their unchristian tyrannical rape, they did not spare the common man, forcing and compelling him contrary to all equity. And this grew out of their pride, blasphemous power, and enterprise. Their rule had to be abolished and rooted out through great war, bloodshed and use of the sword, as is indicated in the Swiss chronicles and many other reliable histories and writings. The conclusion of this pamphlet tells a bit about this. . . .

God can and will no longer tolerate this great misery and wantonness, which is now found everywhere. May God enlighten his poor lambs through divine grace and with true Christian faith, and protect them against these ravaging wolves. . . .

Chapter Five. Which Form of Authority, Hereditary or Elective, Should Be Chosen to Replace the Present Authority?

This subject is much debated on both sides. And a great many insist on the first [form of government, i.e. hereditary or monarchical rule], on the grounds that the natural father takes care of his children much more faithfully than the stepfather. This argument has obvious support; one sees it very clearly in the case of such Christian princes as Frederick of Saxony and Philip, Margrave of Baden, etc.[5]

But, on the other hand, if one looks through Scripture and considers the matter precisely, one finds in truth that immeasurable, unspeakable, and terrible misery and grief have arisen from hereditary authorities. And why should we think of ancient tyrannical deeds? What is still more terrible is that now, in our age, because of greed and pomp, the pure word of God is completely and blasphemously suppressed with the use of prison, torture, and similarly arrogant actions, and violence. And what may the godless, blasphemous, hereditary authorities not do to their subjects! When the Romans ruled with guild masters and a council in a communal government [i.e., a republic], the might of their great

---

[4] An apparent reference to Luther, who was an Augustinian friar.

[5] The Elector Frederick the Wise of Saxony (d. May 5, 1525) was the protector of Luther; Margrave Philip of Baden acted as a mediator between rebellious peasants and princes in the southwestern part of the empire. Since the work speaks of Frederick the Wise as though he were living, it must have been written before mid-May, when knowledge of his death would have become general.

authority over the whole world increased daily. But when lust enticed and led them to fall away from communal government, and they began to set up kings as their own lords, then all their misfortune soon began and the destruction of their empire as well. . . .

Now, in our age, whoever does not gorge, guzzle, or feast, and is not always fuller than a full, puking dog, is not held to be a man. But their rule is held to be so Christian that in justice it should produce happiness. What should I say about this? It is best that I say nothing. . . .

In sum, as soon as the Romans fell from a communal [i.e., republican] government to emperors, all their miseries began and remained among them until they became poor serfs, they whose power had previously ruled mightily over all the world. I am showing all this here only because the great lords all usually pride themselves on their ancient, preeminent descent from Rome. Yes, they pride themselves on an ancient, heathen descent. And they do not consider that we are all descended from God, and that nobody is a minute older in his lineage than anyone else, be he king or shepherd, etc. This [concern about descent] is only a poisonous puffing up of a clod of earth [from which Adam was created]. Adam is the father of us all, and we will all certainly, in one part of us [i.e., the body], fall apart again into rotten pieces of earth. The other part, the soul, will be the booty of either the devil or God. Look, what will you now make of yourself? . . .

In sum, [hereditary rule] is not Christian. The fundamental and true root of all idolatry is the unlimited power of hereditary rulers, which had its origins in Babylon under the first established king, Ninus or Nimrod.[6] . . .

Furthermore, when that elect race, the children of God, the Israelites, had a communal government and no king, then God dwelled cordially among them, and they ruled in a praiseworthy way and lived blessedly. But then heathen desire also enticed and charmed them to establish a powerful king among them, and they bade the prophet Samuel to obtain a king for them from God, as is clearly shown in 1 Samuel 8. God was greatly displeased by this and he foretold great misery and grief, with serfdom and other things which would bind their hands as a result of the power of hereditary kings. These things they then repeatedly experienced. . . .

---

[6] The author equates Ninus and Nimrod; Ninus was the legendary founder of the Assyrian empire, which extended from Egypt to India, and the spouse of Semiramis, who had him murdered around 2000 BCE. For Nimrod, see Gen. 10:8–12.

Chapter Six. Whether Game Belongs to the Common Man or Not

... Christian faith cannot tolerate the godless, unprincely system and government in which a lord appropriates game for himself. In short, he is robbing the poor of what is theirs. For game is free to everyone who catches it on his property. Indeed, another thing is still more important. Every Christian who sees game damaging his neighbor's land is obligated out of Christian brotherly love to drive out the animal which is damaging the community, to protect his neighbor from harm, be this by spearing or shooting it, as he can and may. For a harmful animal is good for nothing except being killed immediately! ...

Here one sees, as in many other acts, how much justice or fear of God is in this limitless insolent power! Yes, but they want to cover up their powerless, rotten evil, their unchristian deeds, with a wordy cloak, and they dare to say that they are not punishing anyone on account of his having hunted game but because he is a disobedient transgressor and a despiser of their commandments. Look here! Look here, dear tightened *Bundschuh* [politically organized peasants], at what a heavy charge is leveled against you! Now you should explode [in anger]. ...

Chapter Seven. Whether a Community May Depose Its Authorities or Not

Now to the heart of the matter! God wants it! Now the storm bells will be sounded! Now the truth must come out, in this time of grace, Luke 19[:11], even if the cliffs should speak [cf. Lk. 19:40]. May the almighty lord and God, and also your pleas, protect me from the intentions of the lords, to say nothing of their desire to do me in. ...

I will speak only briefly about this. All the lords who issue selfish commands stemming from the desires of their hearts and their willful, unjust heads, and who appropriate for themselves—I will remain silent about their plunder—taxes, customs, payments, and what similarly serves the common fund for the protection and maintenance of the common territory, these lords are in truth the real robbers and the declared enemies of their own territory.

Now, to knock people such as Moab, Agag, Ahab, and Nero from their thrones is God's highest pleasure. Scripture does not call them servants of God, but instead snakes, dragons and wolves. Go to it! ...

I will prove that a territory or community has the power to depose its pernicious lords by introducing ... sayings drawn from divine law, which the gates of hell with all their knights cannot destroy. Whoever wants to, can attempt to dispute me. I expect this. But he should tell lies in private, so that he does not betray himself, as do the papists. What would they not give now to have followed Luther in his first true admonition in the *Booklet on the Papacy*?[7] Then they could have rested. Many thoughts would have stayed in their pens which now no one will allow to be scraped or scratched away. . . .

And the first saying from divine law [to prove that a community may depose its lords] is this. Joshua 1[:7f.] commands the principle that no lord has the power to act according to his own will, but only on the basis of divine law. If he does not, simply get rid of him and leave him far behind. This is most pleasing to God. St. Paul provides us the second saying from divine law in 2 Corinthians 10[:8], where he says, "Power is given to build up and not to destroy." And what does St. Paul intend with his punishing and mocking words other than that a harmful ruler should not be tolerated? . . .

Behold! Should a condemned Antichrist then rule the people of Christ, whom the lord of heaven and earth purchased so dearly with his bitter death? What a great need there is to reflect seriously on these words of the divine spirit! . . .

Thus, in any case, we Christians have sufficiently sound and sincere reasons [to depose our lords], and we are also obliged to redeem ourselves from these godless lords out of this Babylonian captivity, as St. Peter says, Acts 5[:29], "We must obey God rather than men." And earlier the divine chancellor, Paul, says in 1 Corinthians 7[:21], "If you are a slave, you can make yourself free, so take the chance." The fourth divine jurist, Matthew, writes in chapter 7[:6], "Do not give what is holy to dogs, nor cast pearls before swine, so that they do not trample these things underfoot, and lest they turn on you and attack you," etc.

Although this divine teaching is twisted in many ways, it is nevertheless based on the true meaning of the [biblical] texts about judges and about the powerful. This teaching makes it evident that neither the law nor the authority of the divine order are a true, holy sanction to evil people. It should be commanded that those whom Christ upbraided here as dogs and swine should be thrown from their thrones! This would be most pleasing to God. . . . From this it follows that—and there

---

[7] Luther's *On the Papacy of Rome, against the Famous Romanists of Leipzig* (*Von den Papstum zu Rome widder den hochberumpten Romanisten zu Leiptzek*), 1520; WA 6, 285ff. The author means that the papists now regret that they did not reach an agreement with Luther based on the principles set forth in this work.

is no other meaning—if a common territory has suffered its lord's arbitrariness and ruination for a long time without hope that he will improve himself, then the common countryside should arm itself boldly with the sword, Luke 17[:1f], and say, "We no longer owe anything to this untrue steward and evil lord." . . .

In sum, let them prattle and gossip about whatever they want. Their power derives ultimately either from the spirit or the flesh. If it derives from the spirit, it is just and most pleasing to God, says Paul to the Romans in chapter 8[:1–8]. But if their authority is derived from the flesh, it is devilish and a most openly declared enemy of God. May God pity us that such fleshly authority should rule over Christian people. And unceasingly they may talk about two kinds of commandments, namely the divine, which concerns the salvation of the soul, and secondly the political, which concerns the common good.[8] Oh God, these commandments cannot be separated from each other. For the political commandments are also divine: truly to further the common good is nothing except truly to maintain brotherly love, which is of the highest merit for blessedness. . . .

And, to silence their snouts a sixth time—from their own secular laws—the pope and emperor do not hold hereditary lordships but elective ones. And they may be deposed, as they often have been, because of their misdeeds. Look! Pope and emperor are also the highest authorities. And should their representatives or lawyers, the princes and other lords, not be deposed on account of their evil rule? . . .

Chapter Eight. In What Form a Community May Depose Its Lords

. . . But if the lords always want to be lords and to treat you poor people in the most arbitrary way, contrary to the divine laws which I have discussed above, then follow Solomon and bravely assemble now! Arm yourselves in the spirit of the bold oxen and steers, who gather together staunchly in a ring with their horns outward, not with the intention of rebelling, but only to defend themselves against the ravaging wolves. In truth, if a wolf is attacking them, he does not get away without cracked ribs, even if he escapes with his life. Thus, you dear brothers, do not

---

[8] A clear reference to Luther's doctrine of the "two realms" or "kingdoms," which he developed in his 1523 tract on secular authority. Here Luther asserted that the authority of secular rulers did not extend to spiritual matters and, conversely, that temporal or secular authority did not pertain to Christian affairs.

engage in this insurrection in order to get rich with other people's prop-erty, or your heart will turn false. Victory will bring you nothing good. You should hate greed as the devil hates the cross! Come together only for the sake of the common peace of the land and to practice Christian freedom! Be united in your goal! . . . [Then,] if your opponents still want to have a war, and they pursue this crazy idea of disputing the gospel with lances, halberds, guns, and armor, then it is God's will. Then let happen what cannot happen differently. Their sacrilegious attacks are hated by God. But you trust in God! Be firm in faith! You are not your own but God's warriors for maintaining the gospel and tearing down the Babylonian prison! Each of you should make every effort to deal with the others in all fidelity and love! Do not quarrel among yourselves and be strict with one another! Let each tolerate the others with the greatest discipline and goodness; maintain the fear of God; and do not tolerate any drinkers! In no case allow blasphemers with their damned tongues among you! Then God will surely be your general.

Chapter Nine. Who Should be Blamed for Being a Rebel?

. . . In sum, they can say whatever they want. No rebellion has ever taken place among the subjects of a Christian lord who rules well. It has only occurred under wastrels and godless tyrants. . . .

Yes, they scream, rant, and curse rebellion so violently, seeking to damn it completely. And in doing this they never think about the cause of the disturbance, which is themselves and their godless nature. Be proud, my dear Sibyl,[9] of your peasants' bound shoe. And even if the lords say more and more, and bring up their ancient lineage, and politely promote their cause, do not be fooled. Old lineage here and old lineage there! The issue is not "ancient lineage" but "rightful lineage"! A thou-sand years of injustice do not make a single hour just. Truly, truly, they will try arguments and tricks, with flattering words and all kinds of clev-erness, whatever they can think up, to make you desert one another. In truth, in truth, "guard yourselves against those who come to you in sheep's clothing but inwardly are ravaging wolves," Matthew 7[:15]. . . .

[9] The Sibyls were prophetesses of ancient Rome. In the Middle Ages an additional prophecy, the so-called Tiburtine Sibyl, was added, which predicted a kingdom of peace and social justice at the end of the world.

Chapter Ten. What Misery and Grief Would Befall the Common Peasantry if They Betray Themselves

Listen, dear brothers. You have embittered the hearts of your lords with overflowing gall so grievously that they can never be sweetened. All thought about mollifying them is in vain. The lords want to be unappeased. They want to be lords, indeed idols, whether this pleases or pains God. . . .

See, this time they will spare you even less. If you do not see through their game, then woe, forever woe, and terrible murder will befall you and the whole peasantry! Oh, woe forever for your children! How can you leave behind such a stepfather's inheritance for them? Look, you must perform labor services with spades, hoes, and horses. Later your children will have to draw the harrow themselves. Up till now you have been able to fence off your holdings against game; from now on you will have to let them stand open. And if up till now your eyes have been gouged out [for poaching], in future you will be impaled. Up till now, if you have paid the heriot, then you are serfs. Henceforth you will become true slaves, with nothing more of your own, neither in body nor in goods. You will be sold completely in the Turkish manner, like cattle, horses, and oxen.

If one of you even turns up his nose against this, then only torture, coercion, and repression will follow from the lords. And there will be no limit to their persecution and slander. . . . And what Christian person would not weep for the miserable grief which you will bring upon yourselves if you are faithless and dishonorable to one another, if you desert one another, and if you do not persevere bravely and brotherly with one another, and stand like Solomon? Since you have been truly warned, do not be foolish! Pay attention and take to heart the kind of murderous misery that occurred nine years ago in Hungary and in the Wendish lands, indeed, before your own door in the "Poor Conrad" [revolt in Württemberg in 1514].[10] And who scattered these peasant troops and brought about this grievous misery? In truth, not by the great number of their enemies but only through their own equivocating disloyalty were the peasants betrayed, taken captive, thrown into the severe Babylonian prison, and given over to sword and axe.

In sum, they would have overcome all this, if they had kept brotherly fidelity with one another, and had not deserted one another. Thus, untruthfulness strikes those who are untruthful.

---

[10] The Hungarian peasant revolt of 1514 under Gyorgy Dozsa, and the 1515 revolt in the Slavic areas of Carniola. For the "Poor Conrad" movement in Württemberg, see Document 3.

Chapter Eleven. An Appropriate Warning to the Aforesaid Christian Brothers

You dear brothers, guard yourselves against such grief, so that among one another you are not deceived, etc. And if one among you in the formation has already set himself up as a great hero, he could certainly be the first to take flight, as I have already warned you most sufficiently above, in chapter eight. And I truly admonish you once again about this: watch out and make sure that no disloyalty arises among you and that no one among you misuses his office. . . . Maintain good order in brotherly unity to prevent such things. . . .

Again, everyone should be diligent and obedient to his authority [in the peasant army]. Hold general assemblies among yourselves often, for nothing strengthens and holds together the common band more heartily.

In the name of Christian order, offer to submit yourselves to the emperor directly and completely, like the other pious imperial cities.

Do not soil your hands with the property of other people unless there is compelling need. Keep all your own goods in moderation, as discussed above and in chapter eight.

But if someone ever wants to exert arbitrary power over you, and will not leave you alone, then the matter must be commended to God [through military conflict]. And let happen what cannot be avoided. . . .

Be sincerely consoled and thankful to God: your great, compelling need, as well as your good reputation and honor have resounded clearly up the Rhine and across the Etsch and Danube. And wherever I travel, far and wide, the prayers of the commoners are heaped on you. On the other hand and without a doubt, the curse of the commoners is heaped with equal vigor on your opponents. The cause will bear fruit, dear brothers, so walk with dignity in this praiseworthy calling.

Hold yourselves solidly together in all fear of God, and brotherly loyalty and love, so that you all become a unified body under the head, Jesus Christ. Then Christ, the true God, will certainly be your general. . . .

And I will remain silent about what is in the old histories: how often great, ineffable deeds have been performed by that poor little band of peasants, your neighbors, the Swiss. How often their enemies have defeated them by boisterous bragging while drinking wine! Then each and every one wants to overcome three Swiss, or wants to defeat them with shepherds and chantry priests. But in most cases their enemies have been put to flight everywhere. And king, emperor, princes, and lords have turned themselves into laughingstocks, no matter how mighty and how well armed was the great armed force they sent into the field against them. And as often as these aforesaid Swiss fought for themselves, for their country, wives, and children, and had to protect themselves from proud power, in most cases they always triumphed and gained great honor. Without a doubt all this has occurred through the power and providence of God. Otherwise, how could the Swiss Confederation, which still increases daily, have grown constantly from only three simple peasants?[11]

And because there is no end to their limitless personal power, and because all the authorities refuse to give us a rest, perhaps the prophecy and the old saying will be fulfilled: "A cow will stand on the Schwanberg mountain in the land of Franconia and low or bellow so loud that it is heard in the middle of Switzerland."[12] In truth, this is not without irony; and in this sense another saying may be fulfilled: "What increases the Swiss but the greed of the lords?" . . .

Thus, you dear brothers, put the greedy desire to get rich with other people's property far from your hearts, or your hearts will have a false foundation. God will not dwell with you. Fight only for what is yours. . . .

But may God, the lord of consolation and patience, grant that you are of one mind among one another, following Jesus Christ in a firm faith, so that unanimously and with one voice you praise God, the father of our lord Jesus Christ. So support one another, just as Christ has supported you, in order to praise God and to gain the protection of his grace, to gain peace here on earth, and to praise his majesty in heaven, so that you may say joyfully with David, Psalm 115[:1], "Not to us, Lord, not to us, but to your name give honor." Amen.

So mobilize yourselves, and do it quickly.
You must do the job, even those of sight that's sickly.

---

[11] An allusion to the legend of the origins of Switzerland in the Oath of Ruetli, a secret association of the first three "confederates," who on the Wednesday before St. Martin's Day 1307 swore to expel the administrative bailiffs on the coming New Year's Day.

[12] The lords of Franconia have generated a rebellion that will be heard about even among the Swiss.

25

Title Page of Against the Murdering and Robbing Hordes of Peasants

May 1525

From mid-April until early May 1525, Luther traveled into the area of the peasant uprising in Saxony and Thuringia. He attempted to calm the peasants with sermons, but his efforts failed. Listeners at Nordhausen responded with heckling and stones. Luther later said that his life was in danger during the trip. When he returned to Wittenberg, he set aside the even-handed view of the rebellion that characterized his Admonition to Peace: A Reply to the Twelve Articles *(Document 22). He now reprinted this tract with an addendum entitled* Against the Murdering and Robbing Hordes of the Other Peasants. *Printers quickly republished this postscript as a separate pamphlet and, as the following image makes clear, dropped the qualifying "other." The tract thus became a general call to repress the rebellion swiftly and with bloodshed.*

The image on the title page shows a pillaging peasant, a sword in one hand and a stolen fowl in the other. The banner above him ironically declares "Love God." The biblical reference beneath the image is to Psalms 7:16, "His mischief will recoil upon himself, and his violence will fall on his own head."

Wider die Mordischen

vnd Reubischen Rotten der Bawren.

hab got lieb

Pfalm: vij.
Seyne tück werden jn selbs treffen/
Vnd seyn mütwill/ wirdt vber jn außgeen.

1 5 2 5.

Martinus Luther, Wittemberg.

26

MARTIN LUTHER

Against the Murdering and Robbing Hordes of Peasants

May 1525

The title page of Luther's most notorious pamphlet against the rebellious peasants (Document 25) shows that the tract was printed as a separate document, not only as an addendum to his Admonition to Peace: A Reply to the Twelve Articles *(Document 22), as he originally composed it. The work's separate printing gave Luther's new condemnation of the peasant rebellion a harsher and more bloodthirsty tone than it would otherwise have had. Nevertheless, Luther did not seek to retract anything contained in the tract. He condemned the rebellious peasants as traitors who had violated their oaths of obedience, as violent felons engaged in robbery and murder, and as blasphemers who falsely claimed a Christian justification for their deeds. He asserted that the rebels merited death on each of these counts, and he urged the princes, both those who were sympathetic to his cause and those who were against evangelical reformation, to crush the insurrection as quickly as possible and with a good conscience. In Luther's view, no crime was worse than rebellion, for it opened the door to all other crimes.*

Against the rioting peasants, Martin Luther.

In my earlier book on this matter,[1] I did not venture to judge the peasants, since they had offered to be corrected and to be instructed. . . . But before I could even inspect the situation, they forgot their promise and violently took matters into their own hands and are robbing and raging like mad dogs. All this now makes it clear that they were trying to deceive us and that the assertions they made in their *Twelve Articles* were nothing but lies presented under the name of gospel. To put it

---

[1] That is, *Admonition to Peace* (Document 22).

Martin Luther, *Luther's Works*, ed. Jaroslav Pelikan and Helmut T. Lehmann, trans. Charles M. Jacobs, rev. Robert C. Schultz (St. Louis: Concordia, 1955–), 46:49–55.

briefly, they are doing the devil's work. This is particularly the work of that archdevil who rules at Mühlhausen[2] and who does nothing except stir up robbery, murder, and bloodshed; as Christ describes him in John 8[:44], "He was a murderer from the beginning." Since these peasants and wretched people have now let themselves be misled and are acting differently than they promised, I, too, must write differently of them than I have written, and begin by setting their sin before them, as God commands Isaiah [58:1] and Ezekiel [2:7], on the chance that some of them may see themselves for what they are. Then I must instruct these rulers how they are to conduct themselves in these circumstances.

The peasants have taken upon themselves the burden of three terrible sins against God and man; by this they have abundantly merited death in body and soul. In the first place, they have sworn to be true and faithful, submissive and obedient, to their rulers, as Christ commands when he says, "Render to Caesar the things that are Caesar's" [Luke 20:25]. And Romans 13[:1] says, "Let every person be subject to the governing authorities." Since they are now deliberately and violently breaking this oath of obedience and setting themselves in opposition to their masters, they have forfeited body and soul, as faithless, perjured, lying, disobedient rascals usually do. . . .

In the second place, they are starting a rebellion, and are violently robbing and plundering monasteries and castles which are not theirs; by this they have doubly deserved death in body and soul as highwaymen and murderers. Furthermore, anyone who can be proved to be a seditious person is an outlaw before God and the emperor; and whoever is the first to put him to death does right and well. For if a man is in open rebellion, everyone is both his judge and his executioner; just as when a fire starts, the first man who can put it out is the best man to do the job. For rebellion is not just simple murder; it is like a great fire, which attacks and devastates a whole land. Thus rebellion brings with it a land filled with murder and bloodshed; it makes widows and orphans, and turns everything upside down, like the worst disaster. Therefore let everyone who can, smite, slay, and stab, secretly or openly, remembering that nothing can be more poisonous, hurtful, or devilish than a rebel. It is just as when one must kill a mad dog; if you do not strike him, he will strike you, and a whole land with you.

In the third place, they cloak this terrible and horrible sin with the gospel, call themselves "Christian brethren," take oaths and submit to

[2] Thomas Müntzer.

them, and compel people to go along with them in these abominations.[3] Thus they become the worst blasphemers of God and slanderers of his holy name. Under the outward appearance of the gospel, they honor and serve the devil, thus deserving death in body and soul ten times over. I have never heard of a more hideous sin. I suspect that the devil feels that the Last Day is coming and therefore he undertakes such an unheard-of act, as though saying to himself, "This is the end, therefore it shall be the worst; I will stir up the dregs and knock out the bottom." God will guard us against him! See what a mighty presence the devil is, how he has the world in his hands. . . .

It does not help the peasants when they pretend that according to Genesis 1 and 2 all things were created free and common, and that all of us alike have been baptized. For under the New Testament, Moses does not count; for there stands our Master, Christ, and subjects us, along with our bodies and our property, to the emperor and the law of this world, when he says, "Render to Caesar the things that are Caesar's" [Luke 20:25]. . . .

For baptism does not make men free in body and property, but in soul; and the gospel does not make goods common, except in the case of those who, of their own free will, do what the apostles and disciples did in Acts 4[:32–37]. They did not demand, as do our insane peasants in their raging, that the goods of others—of Pilate and Herod[4]—should be common, but only their own goods. Our peasants, however, want to make the goods of other men common, and keep their own for themselves. Fine Christians they are! I think there is not a devil left in hell; they have all gone into the peasants. Their raving has gone beyond all measure.

Now since the peasants have brought [the wrath of] both God and man down upon themselves and are already many times guilty of death in body and soul, and since they submit to no court and wait for no verdict, but only rage on, I must instruct the temporal authorities on how they may act with a clear conscience in this matter.

---

[3] Luther is referring to the "Christian union or association" that the peasants at Memmingen created in early March 1525; see "The Memmingen Federal Ordinance" and "The Document of Articles" (Documents 17 and 18), which specified the penalty for failing to join the peasants' association.

[4] In this case, two enemies of Christianity: Pilate, the Roman governor who condemned Jesus to death, and Herod, the king of the Jews who ordered the massacre of the innocents. Luther's point is that neither would have been willing to contribute his property to the common fund of the first Christians, and those Christians would have been wrong to claim it.

First, I will not oppose a ruler who, even though he does not tolerate the gospel, will smite and punish these peasants without first offering to submit the case to judgment. He is within his rights, since the peasants are not contending any longer for the gospel, but have become faithless, perjured, disobedient, rebellious murderers, robbers, and blasphemers, whom even a heathen ruler has the right and authority to punish. Indeed, it is his duty to punish such scoundrels, for this is why he bears the sword and is "the servant of God to execute his wrath on the wrong-doer," Romans 13[:4].

But if the ruler is a Christian and tolerates the gospel, so that the peasants have no appearance of a case against him, he should proceed with fear. First he must take the matter to God, confessing that we have deserved these things, and remembering that God may, perhaps, have thus aroused the devil as a punishment upon all Germany. Then he should humbly pray for help against the devil, for we are contending not only "against flesh and blood," but "against the spiritual hosts of wickedness in the air" [Eph. 6:12, 2:2], which must be attacked with prayer. Then, when our hearts are so turned to God that we are ready to let his divine will be done, whether he will or will not have us to be princes or lords, we must go beyond our duty, and offer the mad peasants an opportunity to come to terms, even though they are not worthy of it. Finally, if that does not help, then swiftly take to the sword.

For in this case a prince and lord must remember that according to Romans 13[:4] he is God's minister and the servant of his wrath and that the sword has been given him to use against such people. If he does not fulfill the duties of his office by punishing some and protecting others, he commits as great a sin before God as when someone who has not been given the sword commits murder. . . . This is not a time to sleep. And there is no place for patience or mercy. This is the time of the sword, not the day of grace.

The rulers, then, should press on and take action in this matter with a good conscience as long as their hearts still beat. It is to the rulers' advantage that the peasants have a bad conscience and an unjust cause, and that any peasant who is killed is lost in body and soul and is eternally the devil's. But the rulers have a good conscience and a just cause. . . .

Thus, anyone who is killed fighting on the side of the rulers may be a true martyr in the eyes of God, if he fights with the kind of conscience I have just described, for he acts in obedience to God's word. On the other hand, anyone who perished on the peasants' side is an eternal firebrand of hell, for he bears the sword against God's word and is disobedient to him, and is a member of the devil. And even if the peasants happen to gain the upper hand (God forbid!) — for to God all things are possible, and we do not know whether it may be his will, through the devil, to destroy all rule and order and cast the world upon a desolate heap, as a prelude to the Last Day, which cannot be far off—nevertheless, those who are found exercising the duties of their office can die without worry and go to the scaffold with a good conscience, and leave the kingdom of this world to the devil and take in exchange the everlasting kingdom. These are strange times, when a prince can win heaven with bloodshed better than other men with prayer!

Finally, there is another thing that ought to motivate the rulers. The peasants are not content with belonging to the devil themselves; they force and compel many good people to join in their devilish league against their wills, and so make them partakers of all of their own wickedness and damnation. . . . Now the rulers ought to have mercy on these prisoners of the peasants, and if they have no other reason to use the sword with a good conscience against the peasants, and to risk their own lives and property in fighting them, this would be reason enough, and more than enough: they would be rescuing and helping these souls whom the peasants have forced into their devilish league and who, without willing it, are sinning so horribly and must be damned. For truly these souls are in purgatory; indeed, they are in the bonds of hell and the devil.

Therefore, dear lords, here is a place where you can release, rescue, help. Have mercy on these poor people! Let whoever can, stab, smite, slay. If you die in doing it, good for you! A more blessed death can never be yours, for you die while obeying the divine word and commandment in Romans 13[:1–2], and in loving service of your neighbor, whom you are rescuing from the bonds of hell and the devil. And so I beg everyone who can to flee from the peasants as from the devil himself; those who do not flee, I pray God will enlighten and convert. As for those who are not to be converted, God grant that they may have neither fortune nor success. To this let every pious Christian say, "Amen!" For this prayer is right and good, and pleases God; this I know. If anyone thinks this too harsh, let him remember that rebellion is intolerable and that the destruction of the world is to be expected every hour.

27

HERMANN MÜHLPFORT, MAYOR OF ZWICKAU

Letter to Stephan Roth at Wittenberg

June 4, 1525

As the insurrection of the common people drew to its bloody conclusion, some began to criticize Luther for the harsh language he used in calling for the merciless slaughter of the rebellious peasants. It is revealing that among these critics was Hermann Mühlpfort, the mayor of Zwickau, an important mining center in southern Saxony near the border of the kingdom of Bohemia. Mühlpfort himself was a good friend of Luther; Luther had in fact dedicated his 1520 tract The Freedom of a Christian *to Mühlpfort. The recipient of Mühlpfort's letter, Stephan Roth, was also close to Luther at Wittenberg. The tone of Mühlpfort's letter showed the dismay within the camp of Luther's followers at what he had written at the height of the rebellion. Mühlpfort pointed out how the common people had turned against Luther, and he predicted that the nobility would now impose new hardships on the poor.*

God be praised, there is peace in and around the city of Zwickau. God help us with his grace. Doctor Martin has fallen into great disfavor with the common people, also with both learned and unlearned: his writing is regarded as having been too fickle. I am greatly moved to write to you about this, for the pastor [Nikolaus Hausmann] and the preachers here have been greatly disconcerted and amazed by the tracts recently issued, since one is clearly contrary to the other. First, [in his *Admonition to Peace*] that Christian man Dr. Martin certainly wrote well, addressing both sides about the danger of princes and peasants jeopardizing their souls' salvation; with God's grace, he certainly expressed a sound judgment with his proposal about how the matter could be mediated, for I, with my limited understanding, knew of no better counsel. But, as I know, the great and powerful would remit to the poor none of

---

Tom Scott and Bob Scribner, eds. and trans., *The German Peasants' War: A History in Documents* (Atlantic Highlands, N.J.: Humanities Press, 1991), 322–24.

the ruinous and intolerable burdens, and may God in heaven take pity on it, for such burdens were contrary to God and all justice.

Afterwards, in a second tract [*A Shocking History and God's Judgment on Thomas Müntzer*], written after he had received a letter from Thomas Müntzer, who so pitiably misled the poor folk, [Luther] became instead the hammer of the poor, without regard for their need, by calling for the poor alone to be quickly destroyed. In the third tract [*Against the Murdering and Robbing Hordes of Peasants*], which I do not consider theological, he called for the private and public murder of the peasants: as long as strength coursed through one's veins, they should be sent to their judgment before God. Is the devil, and those who do this, to be our Lord God? Here I do not agree. In my opinion, there was no pressing need for this hasty tract. There was enough murdering of peasants, burghers, women, and children taking place; not only were the poor folk being killed, but also their goods and possessions were being taken from their innocent wives and children and burnt. God knows, these same knights are supposed to be the children of God! But we should have more pity for the poor, needy, and simple folk who were misled by Thomas and others, and when Thomas Müntzer's letter arrived, [Luther] might have reacted more thoughtfully. . . .

See how violently the nobility will impose all their burdens on the people with the sword and [shed] the blood of the suffering poor, who cannot protect themselves from hunger because of their poverty. But they [the nobility] will rely on Martin's tract, that this [bloodshed] will gain them eternal salvation. If my gracious lord [the elector of Saxony] and other princes had issued a public edict calling for regard for the need of the peasantry, and they had not then disbanded, I would not have had so much pity, but no such thing happened.

Dear Christian brother, who will not speak out about the need of the commons in town and village? Who will have the strength of spirit not to hold back from doing so? Whoever speaks out will be accused of being a rebel and everyone will have to keep silent for fear of tyrants, lest it be said that one is speaking against authority. I know already that in several places more has been imposed upon the poor than before, and they are told openly: "You owe me this; if you do not do it, you are opposing me, who am your lord and have sovereign authority over you." It is said that complaints should be laid before the princes; [but,] yea, I know no one [who] will be a just judge. . . . We can see how some of the nobility kill, stab, and shoot whenever they catch sight of the peasantry. . . . Now I believe that Doctor Martin has good cause to reprove all rebels, for otherwise things would turn out badly. But if the self-interested and the greedy would remit a little to the poor all this would cease. . . .

What has moved me so much to write to you, besides Martin's rash tract, is that poverty has been so much forgotten. I also believe that my pious, Christian territorial princes, young and old, who were certainly innocent of this rebellion and of the bloodshed, could have averted rebellion in their lands if they had exercised control over the nobility, for they have always avoided shedding blood and have not ceased to protect the pious from the wicked. But I fear there will be more disobedience. . . . I fear truly that more violence will erupt and the nobility will increase their arrogance further. There is such boasting and thumping. No one I have seen speaks of kindness and forgiveness; they say everyone will simply be killed, burnt, beheaded who now refuses what they had to render before, whether justly or unjustly, in the way of labor service, grazing, and the like. . . .

Martin has not done well in Zwickau and in the countryside and towns; he has written the truth in condemning rebellion, but the poor have been greatly forgotten. . . . Dated on Whitsun, in the year '25.

28

MARTIN LUTHER

An Open Letter on the Harsh Book against the Peasants

June or July 1525

The publication and distribution of Luther's Against the Murdering and Robbing Hordes of Peasants *(Document 26) coincided with the defeat of the main peasant armies in a series of battles that turned into one-sided slaughters of the rebellious forces. Afterward, some princes and lords also imposed cruel punishments on the survivors—wholesale executions, blindings, maimings, severe fines, and so on. The severity with which the lords suppressed the insurrection led many, such as the Zwickau mayor Hermann Mühlpfort (Document 27) to sympathize with the peasants and to criticize Luther for what they saw as un-Christian harshness toward the peasants. After hesitating, Luther decided to reply to*

Martin Luther, *Luther's Works*, ed. Jaroslav Pelikan and Helmut T. Lehmann, trans. Charles M. Jacobs, rev. Robert C. Schultz (St. Louis: Concordia, 1955–), 46:63–85.

his critics. In the summer of 1525, he wrote and published the following Open Letter *defending his earlier position, retracting nothing of what he had said, and charging his critics with being crypto-rebels in league with the devil.*

To the honorable and wise Casper Müller, chancellor of Mansfield, my good friend. Grace and peace in Christ.

I have been obliged to answer your letter in a printed book because the little book that I published against the peasants has given rise to so many complaints and questions, as though it were un-Christian and too hard. Indeed, I had intended to plug my ears and to let those blind, ungrateful creatures who seek nothing in me but causes of offense smother in their own vexation until they had to rot in it. . . .

First of all, then, I must warn those who criticize my book to hold their tongues and to be careful not to make a mistake and lose their own heads; for they are certainly rebels at heart, and Solomon says, "My son, fear the Lord and the king, and do not be a fellow-traveler with the rebels for their disaster will come suddenly and who can know what ruin of both you and them will be?" Proverbs 24[:21–22]. Thus we see that both rebels and those who join them are condemned. God does not want us to make a joke out of this but to fear the king and the government. Those who are fellow-travelers with rebels sympathize with them, feel sorry for them, justify them, and show mercy to those on whom God has no mercy, but whom he wishes to have punished and destroyed. For the man who thus sympathizes with the rebels makes it perfectly clear that he has decided in his heart that he will also cause disaster if he has the opportunity. The rulers, therefore, ought to shake these people up until they keep their mouths shut and realize that the rulers are serious.

If they think this answer is too harsh, and that this is talking violence and only shutting men's mouths, I reply, "That is right." A rebel is not worth rational arguments, for he does not accept them. You have to answer people like that with a fist, until the sweat drips off their noses. The peasants would not listen; they would not let anyone tell them anything, so their ears must now be unbuttoned with musket balls till their heads jump off their shoulders. Such pupils need a rod. He who will not hear God's word when it is spoken with kindness, must listen to the headsman, when he comes with his axe. If anyone says I am being uncharitable and unmerciful about this, my reply is: This is not a question of mercy, we are talking about God's word. It is God's will that the king be honored and the rebels destroyed; and he is as merciful as we are. . . .

My good friends, you praise mercy so highly because the peasants are beaten; why did you not praise it when the peasants were raging, smiting, robbing, burning, and plundering, in ways that are terrible to see or even to hear about? Why were they not merciful to the princes and lords, whom they wanted to exterminate completely? No one spoke of mercy then. Everything was "rights"; nothing was said of mercy, it was nothing. "Rights, rights, rights!" They were everything. Now that the peasants are beaten, and the stone that they threw at heaven is falling back on their own heads, no one is to say anything of rights, but to speak only of mercy.

And yet they are stupid enough to think that no one notices the rascal behind it! Ah, no! We see you, you black, ugly devil! You praise mercy not because you are seriously concerned about mercy, or you would have praised it to the peasants; on the contrary, you are afraid for your own skin, and are trying to use the appearance and reputation of mercy to escape God's rod and punishment. This will not work, dear fellow! You must take your turn, and die without mercy. . . .

Here you see the intention of those who condemn my book as though it forbade mercy. It is certain that they are either peasants, rebels, bloodhounds themselves, or have been misled by such people; for they would like all wickedness to go unpunished. Thus under the name of mercy they would be—so far as it is in their power—the most merciless and cruel destroyers of the whole world. . . .

[T]he kingdom of the world, which is nothing else than the servant of God's wrath upon the wicked and is a real precursor of hell and everlasting death, should not be merciful, but strict, severe, and wrathful in fulfilling its work and duty. Its tool is not a wreath of roses or a flower of love, but a naked sword; and a sword is a symbol of wrath, severity, and punishment. . . .

Now he who would confuse these two kingdoms—as our false fanatics do—would put wrath into God's kingdom and mercy into the world's kingdom; and that is the same as putting the devil in heaven and God in hell. . . .

My little book was not written against ordinary evildoers, but against rebels. You must make a very, very great distinction between a rebel and a thief, or a murderer, or any other kind of evildoer. . . .

A rebel is a man who runs at his head and lord with a naked sword. No one should wait, then, until his lord commands him to defend him, but the first person who can, ought to take the initiative and run in and stab the rascal, and not worry about committing murder; for he is warding off an arch-murderer, who wants to murder the whole land. Indeed, if he does not thrust and slay, but lets his lord be run through, he, too, is an arch-murderer; for he must then remember that because his lord suffers and is laid low, he is himself in that case, lord, judge, and executioner. Rebellion is no joke, and there is no evil deed on earth that compares with it. Other wicked deeds are single acts; rebellion is a flood of all wickedness.

I am called a clergyman and am a minister of the word, but even if I served a Turk and saw my lord in danger, I would forget my spiritual office and stab and hew as long as my heart beat. If I were slain in so doing, I should go straight to heaven. For rebellion is a crime which deserves neither a court trial nor mercy, whether it be among heathen, Jews, Turks, Christians, or any other people; the rebel has already been tried, judged, condemned, and sentenced to death and everyone is authorized to execute him.

29

ALBRECHT DÜRER

Design for a Monument to the Victory over the Peasants

1525

In the years before his death in 1528 at Nuremberg, the great German Renaissance artist Albrecht Dürer worked on a four-volume treatise on measurements, which was published in 1525. The work included a set of designs for hypothetical monuments. Dürer drew up this proposal for a column to celebrate the victory of the lords over the peasants. At the base of the monument was a group of domesticated animals (oxen, sheep, pigs). The central feature of the monument was a column, near the bottom of which was a plaque with the inscription "The year of our Lord 1525." The column itself was composed of symbols of agricultural labor and its products. Atop the column sat a peasant, head in hand, in the conventional pose of the Man of Sorrows. Most striking of all, from the peasant's back protruded a sword. What Dürer intended with the design is unclear. His interest in the proportions of the various components of the column is evident. But was his intention critical and ironical: to design a "monument" that would demonstrate the betrayal of the peasants' cause, perhaps by Luther, and the injustice of the lords' violent repression of the rebellion? Or did Dürer mean to celebrate the princes' victory over the peasants as a defeat they richly deserved for attempting to usurp the place of the lords as the natural ruling elite of society?

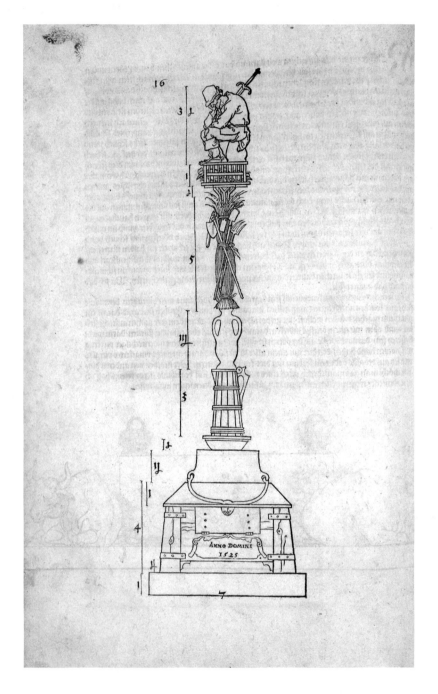

ANNO DOMINI
1525

142

A Chronology of the Early Reformation and the Peasants' War (1502–1526)

1502 Bundschuh conspiracy in Speyer.

1513 Bundschuh conspiracy in Freiburg im Breisgau.

1514 "Poor Conrad" protest movement in Württemberg.

1517 *October 31* Luther's Ninety-Five Theses protesting the sale of indulgences.

1518 Zwingli begins ministry in Zurich.

1519 Charles V elected Holy Roman emperor.

1520 *June* Papal bull warns Luther that he risks excommunication.

August Luther's *To the Christian Nobility of the German Nation* published.

November Luther's *The Freedom of a Christian* published.

December Luther and followers burn papal bull and Catholic writings.

1521 *January* Pope Leo X excommunicates Luther.

April Luther's appearance at Diet of Worms, after which he goes into hiding at Wartburg.

1522 *January* Imperial governing council issues edict prohibiting ecclesiastical innovations.

September Luther's vernacular translation of the New Testament published.

1523 *January 29* Zurich Disputation; Zwingli defends Sixty-Seven Articles.

January–October Consolidation of Reformation in Zurich.

April Müntzer begins reforms at Allstedt.

1524 *May* First peasant risings in Forchheim, Franconia, and the Black Forest.

June Peasant protest at Stühlingen in the Upper Rhine.

July 13 Müntzer preaches "Sermon to the Princes" at Allstedt castle.

August 19 Müntzer and Pfeiffer lead rebellion in Mühlhausen in Thuringia.

1525 *February 24* Battle of Pavia and victory of Charles V.

March 6 Peasant "parliament" at Memmingen leads to formation of Christian Association of Lake of Constance, Allgäu, and Baltringen bands on basis of the "Memmingen Federal Ordinance."

March 19 First printing of *The Twelve Articles of the Upper Swabian Peasants.*

April 1 Peasant revolt in bishopric of Würzburg; formation of Tauber Valley peasant band in Franconia.

April 2 Peasant uprising in Neckar Valley.

April 14 Peasant rebellion in Alsace; formation of Bildhausen band in region of Franconia.

April 16 Peasant uprising in duchy of Württemberg.

April 17 Treaty of Weingarten between Swabian League and peasants of Württemberg and Franconia.

April 19 Luther's *Admonition to Peace: A Reply to the Twelve Articles of the Peasants of Swabia.*

April 23 Peasant uprisings in the Palatinate of the Rhine and Switzerland.

April 26–27 Urban revolts in Mainz and Cologne; Müntzer writes letter to League of the Elect at Allstedt.

April 28 Peasants occupy city of Erfurt.

May 2 Peasant revolt in Baden.

May 5 Luther's *Against the Murdering and Robbing Hordes of the Other Peasants* published at Wittenberg.

May 8 Black Forest band presents "Document of Articles" to city of Villingen; peasants capture Würzburg and lay siege to bishop's fortress of Frauenburg.

May 9 Peasant uprising in the Tirol.

Mid-May Publication of *To the Assembly of the Common Peasantry* at Nuremberg.

May 12   Battle of Böblingen and defeat of peasants of Württemberg.

May 15   Battle of Frankenhausen and defeat of peasants of Thuringia.

May 17   Battle of Saverne and defeat of peasants of Alsace.

May 27   Execution of Müntzer outside Mühlhausen.

June 2   Battle of Königshofen and defeat of Odenwald peasants.

June 4   Hermann Mühlpfort writes letter to Stephan Roth at Wittenberg; battle of Ingolstadt and end of rising in Franconia.

June–July   Luther publishes *Open Letter on the Harsh Book against the Peasants.*

September 3   Peasant uprising in Prussia.

1526   *February*   Gaismair's "Territorial Constitution for the Tirol."

March   Renewed uprisings in bishopric of Salzburg.

June–August   Imperial Diet at Speyer considers peasants' grievances; grants some reforms.

Questions for Consideration

1. What socioeconomic changes in the Holy Roman Empire in the late fifteenth and early sixteenth centuries led many people to feel anxiety and discontent?

2. In what ways were the grievances and conspiracies of the pre-Reformation peasantry, however much they revolved around economic issues, also expressed in religious terms (see Documents 1 and 3)? What religious values and ideas were important to the peasantry?

3. At the outset of the Reformation, did Martin Luther limit his challenge to authority and his call for reform to the church alone? What other concerns animated his writings? What was Luther's idea of Christian freedom (see Documents 6, 8, and 11)?

4. In what ways were the political views of Huldrych Zwingli different from those of Martin Luther (compare Documents 6, 8, and 10)?

5. Did Thomas Müntzer present a more radical vision of both religion and politics than that of either Martin Luther or Huldrych Zwingli (compare Document 12 with Documents 8 and 10)?

6. In what ways did Luther's and Zwingli's principles about how the church should be reformed influence the authors of *The Twelve Articles* (compare in particular Document 14 with Documents 10 and 11)?

7. Does it make sense to distinguish between purely religious and purely secular demands in the program of *The Twelve Articles* (see Document 14)? In the eyes of the peasants, were all the changes they sought what was needed to live according to the Word of God?

8. How did the peasants' actions support or contradict their initial disclaimers that their understanding of the gospel was not a cause of violence, that they were willing to accept instruction about divine law, that they were willing to negotiate regarding many of their demands, and so on (see especially Documents 14 and 24)?

9. What connected the constitutional principles formulated by radical reformers such as Thomas Müntzer and Balthasar Hubmaier and the political organizations and policies of the rebellious peasants (examine Documents 15, 17, and 18)?

10. Were the values and principles the commoners expressed during the Peasants' War influenced by the early Reformation, or were they the same as those expressed by the peasants prior to Luther's protest?

11. Despite the great violence of the commoners' insurrection, to what extent did their organizational efforts and field ordinances also show that they wanted to proceed in a deliberate and orderly manner (see in particular Documents 17–19)?

12. To what extent may we describe the political principles and social ideals that animated Michael Gaismair's constitution for the Tirol (see Document 21) as "proto-democratic" and "proto-modern"? Did Gaismair's principles and ideals also contain features that were neither democratic nor modern?

13. To what extent were the constitutional principles that some parties in the rebellion asserted republican principles (see in particular Documents 15, 21, and 24)?

14. Was Martin Luther guilty of hypocrisy in his attitude toward the commoners and his response to the insurrection, as his Roman Catholic critics charged (see Document 7)? That is, did Luther first encourage the commoners to reject authority and then condemn them for having done so (compare Documents 8, 11, and 22)?

15. In what ways did the author of *To the Assembly of the Common Peasantry* (see Document 24) reply to Luther's condemnation of rebellion by the common people (as set forth in Documents 8 and 22)? On what points did the author agree with Luther's view of secular politics, and where did he disagree?

16. Was the justification for using violence to overthrow the existing authorities, as set forth in *To the Assembly of the Common Peasantry* (Document 24), more in line with the political ideas of Thomas Müntzer (Documents 12 and 15) or Huldrych Zwingli (Document 10)?

17. Why did Luther not only view the Peasants' War as the work of the devil but also charge anyone who sympathized with the rebellious peasants with being an agent of the devil (Documents 26 and 28)?

18. Assuming a historical counterfactual—that the insurrection of the commoners had succeeded and their goals had been realized—how might German politics and society in the early modern period have looked?

Selected Bibliography

SOCIOECONOMIC LIFE AND DISCONTENT PRIOR TO THE REFORMATION

Blickle, Peter. *From the Communal Reformation to the Revolution of the Common Man*. Leiden: Brill, 1998.

———. *Obedient Germans? A Rebuttal: A New View of German History*, trans. Thomas A. Brady Jr. Charlottesville: University of Virginia Press, 1997.

———. "Peasant Revolts in the German Empire in the Late Middle Ages." *Social History* 4 (1979): 223–39.

Brady, Thomas A., Jr. *German Histories in the Age of Reformations, 1400–1650*. Cambridge: Cambridge University Press, 2009.

Dykema, Peter, and Heiko A. Oberman, eds. *Anticlericalism in the Late Middle Ages and the Reformation*. Leiden: E. J. Brill, 1993.

Huppert, George. *After the Black Death: A Social History of Early Modern Europe*. Bloomington: Indiana University Press, 1986.

Scott, Tom. *Freiburg and the Breisgau: Town-Country Relations in the Age of the Reformation and the Peasants' War*. Oxford: Clarendon, 1986.

———. "The German Peasants' War and the 'Crisis of Feudalism': Reflections on a Neglected Theme." *Journal of Early Modern History* 6 (2002): 265–95.

———. *Regional Identity and Economic Change: The Upper Rhine, 1450–1600*. New York: Oxford University Press, 1997.

———. *Society and Economy in Germany, 1300–1600*. New York: Palgrave, 2002.

———. *Town, Country, and Regions in Reformation Germany*. Leiden: Brill, 2005.

Sreenivasan, Govind P. "The Social Origins of the Peasants' War of 1525 in Upper Swabia." *Past and Present* 171 (May 2001): 30–65.

Scribner, Bob, ed. *Germany: A New Social and Economic History*, Vol. 1, *1450–1630*. London: Arnold, 1996.

Sea, Thomas F. "The Swabian League and Peasant Disobedience before the German Peasants' War." *Sixteenth Century Journal* 30 (1999): 89–111.

THE EARLY REFORMATION MOVEMENTS

Blickle, Peter. *Communal Reformation: The Quest for Salvation in Sixteenth Century Germany*, trans. Thomas Dunlap. Atlantic Highlands, N.J.: Humanities Press, 1992. First German ed. 1987.

Brady, Thomas A. *Communities, Politics and Reformation in Early Modern Europe*. Leiden: Brill, 1998.

Chadwick, Owen, ed. *The Early Reformation on the Continent*. New York: Oxford University Press, 2001.

Chrisman, Miriam Usher. *Conflicting Visions of Reform: German Lay Propaganda Pamphlets, 1519–1530*. Atlantic Highlands, N.J.: Humanities Press, 1996.

Dixon, C. Scott, ed. *The German Reformation: The Essential Readings*. Oxford: Blackwell, 1999.

———. *The Reformation in Germany*. Oxford: Oxford University Press, 2002.

Edwards, Mark U., Jr. *Printing, Propaganda and Martin Luther*. Berkeley: University of California Press, 1994.

Estes, James S. *Peace, Order and the Glory of God: Secular Authority and the Church in the Thought of Luther and Melanchthon, 1518–1559*. Leiden: Brill, 2005.

Hsia, R. Po-Chia, ed. *The German People and the Reformation*. Ithaca, N.Y.: Cornell University Press, 1988.

Matheson, Peter. *The Rhetoric of the Reformation*. Edinburgh: T. and T. Clark, 1998.

Moxey, Keith. *Peasants, Warriors, and Wives: Popular Imagery in the Reformation*. Chicago: University of Chicago Press, 1989.

Oberman, Heiko. *Luther: Man Between God and the Devil*, trans. Eileen Walliser-Schwarzbart. New Haven, Conn.: Yale University Press, 1990.

Ozment, Steven E. *The Reformation in the Cities*. New Haven, Conn.: Yale University Press, 1975.

Potter, G. R. *Zwingli*. Cambridge: Cambridge University Press, 1976.

Scribner, R. W. *For the Sake of Simple Folk: Popular Propaganda for the German Reformation*. 2nd ed. Oxford: Oxford University Press, 1994.

———. *Popular Culture and Popular Movements in Reformation Germany*. London: Hambledon, 1987.

———. *Varieties of Reformation*. London: Historical Association, 1993.

Scribner, R. W., and C. Scott Dixon. *The German Reformation*. 2nd ed. New York: Palgrave, 2003.

Wandel, Lee Palmer. *Voracious Idols and Violent Hands: Iconoclasm in Reformation Zurich, Strasbourg and Basel*. Cambridge: Cambridge University Press, 1995.

THE PEASANTS' WAR

Blickle, Peter. *From the Communal Reformation to the Revolution of the Common Man*, trans. Beat Kümin. Leiden: Brill, 1998.

————. *The Revolution of 1525: The German Peasants' War from a New Perspective,* trans. Thomas A. Brady Jr. and H. C. Erik Midelfort. Baltimore: Johns Hopkins University Press, 1981. First German edition, Munich: R. Oldenbourg, 1977; 4th ed., 2007.

Cohn, Henry J. "Anticlericalism in the German Peasants' War." *Past and Present* 83 (1979): 3–31.

Engels, Friedrich. *The German Revolutions: "The Peasant War in Germany" and "Germany: Revolution and Counter-Revolution,"* ed. Leonard Krieger. Chicago: University of Chicago Press, 1967.

Goertz, Hans-Jürgen. *Thomas Müntzer: Apocalyptic, Mystic and Revolutionary,* trans. Jocelyn Jaquiery, ed. Peter Matheson. Edinburgh: T. and T. Clark, 1993.

Kirchner, Hubert. *Luther and the Peasants' War,* trans. Darrell Jodock. Philadelphia: Fortress, 1972.

Kolb, Robert. "The Theologians and the Peasants. Conservative Evangelical Reactions to the German Peasants Revolt." *Archiv für Reformationsgeschichte* 69 (1978): 103–31.

Miller, Douglas, and Angus McBride (illus.). *Armies of the German Peasants' War 1524–26.* Oxford: Osprey, 2003.

Porter, J. M. "Luther and Political Millenarianism: The Case of the Peasants' War." *Journal of the History of Ideas* 42 (1981): 389–406.

Scott, Tom, and Bob Scribner, eds. and trans. *The German Peasants' War: A History in Documents.* Atlantic Highlands, N.J.: Humanities Press, 1991.

Scott, Tom. "The Peasants' War," in R. Po-Chia Hsia, ed., *A Companion to the Reformation World.* Malden, Mass.: Blackwell, 2004, 56–69.

————. "The Peasants' War: A Historiographical Review." Parts I and II. *The Historical Journal* 22 (1979): 693–720, 953–74.

————. *Thomas Müntzer: Theology and Revolution in the German Reformation.* New York: St. Martin's Press, 1989.

Scribner, Bob, and Gerhard Benecke, eds. *The German Peasant War of 1525: New Viewpoints.* London: George Allen & Unwin, 1979.

Sea, Thomas F. "Imperial Cities and the Peasants' War in Germany." *Central European History* 12 (1979): 3–37.

Stayer, James M. *The German Peasants' War and Anabaptist Community of Goods.* Montreal: McGill-Queen's University Press, 1991.

Vice, Roy L. "Ehrenfried Krump, Karlstadt's Patron and Peasant's War Rebel." *Archive for Reformation History* 86 (1995): 153–74.

————. "Iconoclasm in Rothenburg ob der Tauber in 1525." *Archiv für Reformationsgeschichte* 89 (1998): 55–78.

————. "The Leadership and Structure of the Tauber Band during the Peasants' War in Franconia." *Central European History* 21 (1988): 175–95.

Acknowledgments (continued from p. iv)

Documents 1 and 3: *Manifestations of Discontent on the Eve of the Reformation*, Gerald Strauss, ed. Copyright © 1971 Indiana University Press, Bloomington, pp. 144–47 and 151–53. Reprinted with permission of Indiana University Press.

Document 2: Pamphilius Gegenbach, *Der Bundschuh* (1514). Bayerische Staatsbibliothek München, Rar. 1677#Beibd.7, title page.

Document 4: From *Luther's Works*, Volume 31, copyright © Fortress Press, copyright © 2011 Evangelical Lutheran Church in America, admin. Augsburg Fortress Publishers. Reproduced by permission. All rights reserved.

Document 5: Hans J. Hillerbrand, ed., *The Reformation: A Narrative History Related by Contemporary Observers and Participants*. © Hans J. Hillerbrand/SCM Press, 1964, pp. 80–84. Reproduced by permission of Hymns Ancient & Modern Ltd. (London).

Document 6: From *Luther's Works*, Volume 44, copyright © Fortress Press, copyright © 2011 Evangelical Lutheran Church in America, admin. Augsburg Fortress Publishers. Reproduced by permission. All rights reserved.

Document 7: "Den Bundschuhschmieren"; woodcut in: Murner, Thomas: *Von demgrossen Lutherischen Narrenwie in doctor Murner beschworen hat* (Straßburg, 1522). Bayerische Staatsbibliothek München, Rar. 870, title page and woodcut.

Document 8: From *Luther's Works*, Volume 45, copyright © Fortress Press, copyright © 2011 Evangelical Lutheran Church in America, admin. Augsburg Fortress Publishers. Reproduced by permission. All rights reserved.

Document 9: "Der Ablasskrämer," Burgerbibliothek Bern, Mss.h.h.XVI.159, f. 2r.

Document 10: Huldrych Zwingli, *Writings*, vol. 1: *The Defense of the Reformed Faith*, trans. E. J. Furcha (Allison Park, Pa.: Pickwick Publications, 1984), pp. 260–82. Used by permission of Wipf and Stock Publishers. www.wipfandstock.com.

Document 11: From *Luther's Works*, Volume 39, copyright © Fortress Press, copyright © 2011 Evangelical Lutheran Church in America, admin. Augsburg Fortress Publishers. Reproduced by permission. All rights reserved.

Documents 12, 17, 18, 21, and 24: *The Radical Reformation*, edited and translated by Michael Baylor. Copyright © 1991 Cambridge University Press. Reprinted with permission.

Document 13, 19, and 27: Reprinted from *The German Peasants' War*, edited and translated by Tom Scott and Bob Scribner (Amherst, N.Y.: Humanity Books, 1998), pp. 65–72, 160–63, and 322–24. Copyright © 1991 by Tom Scott and Bob Scribner. All rights reserved. Reprinted with permission of the publisher; www.prometheusbooks.com.

Document 16: *Handlung, Artickel und Instruction so fürgenommen sein worden von allen Rotten und Hauffen den Bawern* (1525). Sächsische Landesbibliothek - Staats- und Universitätsbibliothek Dresden (SLUB), Hist.Germ.B.178,48 – Titelblatt.

Document 20: Michael G. Baylor, ed. and trans., *Revelation and Revolution: Basic Writings of Thomas Müntzer* (Bethlehem, Pa.: Lehigh University Press, 1993), pp. 190–92. Reprinted with permission of Associated University Presses.

Documents 22, 26, and 28: From *Luther's Works*, Volume 46, copyright © Fortress Press, copyright © 2011 Evangelical Lutheran Church in America, admin. Augsburg Fortress Publishers. Reproduced by permission. All rights reserved.

Document 23: Herzog August Bibliothek Wolfenbüttel: 189.27 Theol. (126).

Document 25: Martin Luther, *Wider die mordischen und reubischen Rotten der Bawren* (1525). Bayerische Staatsbibliothek München, Res/Germ.sp. 671 n, title page.

Document 29: Museen der Stadt Nuernberg - Graphische Sammlung (Albrecht-Dürer-Haus-Stiftung).

Index

"About the Great Lutheran Fool"
(Murner), 55
"Actions, Articles and Instructions That All
the Platoons and Bands of the Peasants
Have Obligated Themselves to Carry
Out, 1525," 85–86
"Admonition to Peace: A Reply to the Twelve
Articles" (Luther), 26, 106–13, 144
"Against the Murdering and Robbing
Hordes of Peasants" (Luther), 28–29,
128–34, 137, 144
title page of, 128–29
Allstedt rebellion, 13, 68, 98
Anabaptists, 30
anticlericalism
in early rebellions, 7
Luther's response to violence of, 57–59
Reformation and, 10, 12
violence and, 11, 19, 24, 36, 37, 57, 59–60
"Arise, O Lord" (Pope Leo X), 46–49
Aristotelian philosophy, 8
"Articles of the *Bundschuh* in the Bishopric
of Speyer, The," 35–38
"Articles of the Peasants of Stühlingen,"
74–75
Augustinian order, 8

"Babylonian Captivity of the Church, The"
(Luther), 50
bands. *See Haufens* (bands)
Battle of Pavia, 27, 144
Bavaria, 6
Black Forest rebellion, 15, 16–17, 38, 74,
90, 144
Blickle, Peter, 21, 22, 115
Böhm, Hans, 7–8
Bright Band field ordinance, 93–97
Bruchsal, *Bundschuh* conspiracy in, 35–36
Bund (political unions), 24–26
Christian egalitarianism and, 24–25
"The Constitutional Draft" and, 83–84
"The Document of Articles," 90–92, 144

formation of territorial unions, 25–26
Gaismair's territorial constitution for the
Tirol, 100–105
Memmingen Federal Ordinance, 85–89, 144
Müntzer's secret union, 13, 68
religious function of, 24
worldly ban and, 90–92
Bundschuh, 8, 24, 35
Bundschuh conspiracies, 7–8, 21, 55
in bishopric of Speyer, 35–38, 143
"Poor Conrad" movement, 40–42, 143
title page of pamphlet describing, 38–39

Calvinist rebellions, 19
capitalist entrepreneurs
Gaismair's attempted reform of, 104–5
growth of, 5
Luther's attack on, 53
mining industry, 5, 20, 101, 104–5
Charles V, 10, 27, 46–47, 143, 144
Christian egalitarianism
Luther on, 9, 50, 51–52, 112
peasant uprising and, 14–15
political unions and, 24–25
rejection of clerical privileges and, 12, 50
cities
"free imperial," 6
peasantry's view of, 5
rebellions in, 15–16, 20
reform movement in, 11–12, 13
clergy
communal right to choose, 13, 66, 67–68,
77–78
Luther's blame of rebellions on, 26, 106,
107–8, 110, 111, 131
Luther's rejection of authority of, 1, 9, 10,
12, 50–53, 67–68
moral depravity of, 7
participation in Peasants' War, 19–20, 23,
76, 83, 98–100
as secular rulers, 2, 3
See also anticlericalism

clerical reformers, 10, 11–12
communal institutions
    early growth of, 4
    Haufens (bands), 22–25
    political unions, 24–26, 83–92
    right to appoint pastors, 13, 66, 67–68,
        77–78
    rural communes, 14
    social and political tensions in, 14–15
    Zwingli's view of powers of, 13, 61–65
    See also Bund (political unions); *Haufens*
        (bands); republicanism
communal lands, grievances about, 42, 81
communal reformation, Luther's program-
    matic principles for, 13, 65–68
Constantinople, 7
"Constitutional Draft, The" (Müntzer, Hub-
    maier), 83–84, 90

"Design for a Monument to the Victory over
    the Peasants" (Dürer), 140–42
Deutsch, Niklaus Manuel, 59
Diet of Worms, 10, 143
disaster prophecies, 7
"Disputation on the Power and Efficacy of
    Indulgences" (Luther), 43
"Document of Articles, The," 90–92, 144
Dominican order, 46
Dürer, Albrecht, "Design for a Monument to
    the Victory over the Peasants," 140–42

economic factors. *See* socioeconomic factors

"Field Ordinances of the Franconian Peas-
    antry, The," 93–97
Franconia rebellion, 6, 7–8, 20, 93, 144
Frederick the Wise of Saxony, 10, 29, 46, 119
"Freedom of a Christian, The" (Luther),
    50, 143
Fritz, Joss, 35–36, 40

Gaismair, Michael, 21
    "Territorial Constitution for the Tirol,"
        100–105, 145
Gegenbach, Pamphilus, 38–39
Georg of Waldburg, 27
Geyer, Florian, 19
gospel
    commoners' government based on, 17,
        83–89
    peasant rebellions based on, 21–22, 76–77
    Reformation and, 10–11
"Greasing the Bundschuh," 55–56

Habsburg dynasty, 8
Haufens (bands), 22–25
    field ordinance of Bright Band, 93–97
    as military formation, 23–24
    political identity of, 24–26
    regional identity of, 22–23
    See also Bund (political unions)
Herolt, Johann, 23

Holy Roman Empire
    in early sixteenth century, 2
    "free imperial cities" in, 6
    growing discontent and unrest in, 6–8,
        35–36
    power of territorial principalities, 5–6, 7
    response to early reform literature, 7
    Turkish threat to, 6–7
Hubmaier, Balthasar, 16, 17
    "The Constitutional Draft," 83–84
Hungary, 7
hunting grievances, 41, 79–80, 112, 121
Hussite rebellion, 19

iconoclasm, 11, 24, 57, 68
"Indulgence Seller, The" (Deutsch), 59
indulgences, sale of, 1, 7, 8, 43–46
inheritance patterns, 5

laity
    evangelical reform and, 10
    participation in Peasants' War, 20
    reformers' view of, 11
land speculation, 5
landlords
    economic expansion and, 4
    as petty princes, 6
    reformation literature on, 7
    See also serfdom
Landschaft formation, 25
League of the Elect, 68, 98, 144
"Letter to Stephan Roth at Wittenberg"
    (Mühlpfort), 135–37
"Letter to the League at Allstedt" (Müntzer),
    98–100, 144
literacy, 12, 14
Lotzer, Sebastian, "The Twelve Articles of
    the Upper Swabian Peasants," 76–82
Luther, Martin
    "Admonition to Peace: A Reply to the
        Twelve Articles," 26, 106–13, 144
    "Against the Murdering and Robbing
        Hordes of Peasants," 28–29, 128–34,
        144
    attempt to calm rebelling peasants, 128
    blame of rebellions on nobility, 26, 106,
        107–8
    burning of papal writings, 10, 143
    cautions against unlawful violence, 3, 12,
        57–59
    communal reformation and, 13, 65–68
    condemnation of peasant violence, 26, 27,
        106, 108–11, 112–13, 128–34, 137–40
    critics of, 13, 55–56, 68, 135–37
    excommunication of, 1, 9, 10, 143
    initiation of Reformation, 1, 8–10, 43–44
    "Ninety-Five Theses," 1, 43–46, 143
    "An Open Letter on the Harsh Book
        against the Peasants," 137–40, 145
    papal condemnation of, 9, 10, 46–49, 67
    rejection of clerical authority, 9, 10, 12,
        50–53, 67–68

response to critics, 137–40
"The Rights of a Christian Congregation,"
  65–68
on role of nobility in spiritual reforms,
  12–13, 29–30, 50–54
"A Sincere Admonition to Guard against
  Rebellion," 57–59
support of princes' repressive violence,
  28–29, 130–34
"To the Christian Nobility of the German
  Nation," 7, 50–54, 143
vernacular translation of Bible, 10, 143
Zwingli's key differences from, 13, 61

Medici, Giovanni de', 46
"Memmingen Federal Ordinance, The," 25,
  85–89, 90, 144
  title page of, 85–86
merchants/craftsmen
  support of Peasants' War, 20
  urban, support of reformers, 12
mining industry
  Gaismair's reforms for, 101, 102, 104–5
  peasant uprisings and, 20, 99
  workers' grievances, 5
Mühlhausen rebellion, 15, 98, 144
Mühlpfort, Hermann, 138
  "Letter to Stephan Roth at Wittenberg,"
    135–37
Müller, Hans, 16
Müntzer, Thomas
  capture and death of, 27, 145
  "The Constitutional Draft," 83–84
  "Letter to the League at Allstedt," 98–100
  preaching to insurgents, 17
  rebellion in Mühlhausen and, 15, 144
  sanction of active resistance, 13–14,
    69–73, 98–100
  "Sermon to the Princes," 68–73, 144
  vernacular liturgy of, 13, 68
Murner, Thomas, 55

"Ninety-Five Theses" (Luther), 1, 43–46,
  143
nobility
  defeat of peasants, 27–29, 137
  economic conditions favoring, 4
  initial concessions to peasants, 17, 27
  lesser, joining with peasants, 19
  Luther on authority to institute reforms,
    12–13, 29–30, 50–54, 65–68
  Luther's blame of rebellions on, 26, 106,
    107–8
  Luther's support of repressive violence of,
    28–29, 130–34
  Müntzer's sermon to, 68–73
  opposing Reformation, 13, 65
  See also secular authority

"Open Letter on the Harsh Book against the
  Peasants, An" (Luther), 137–40, 145
Ottoman Turks, 7

papacy
  denouncement of Luther, 1, 9, 10, 46–49,
    143
  Luther's attack on, 1, 8–10, 43–46, 50–53,
    67
  taxation and fees of, 7
peasantry
  anticlerical violence and, 59–60
  economic downturn for, 4–5
  grievances of, 16, 40–42, 74–75,
    78–82
  groups included in, 20
  hostility toward merchant-capitalists, 5
  late medieval market advantages for, 4
  oral culture of, 14
  pre-Reformation uprisings, 7–8, 35–42
"Peasants Torturing an Indulgence
  Preacher," 59–60
Peasants' War
  aftermath of, 29–30, 138
  aims of, 20–22
  approaches to political reform, 25–26
  in cities, 15–16, 20
  clerical sympathizers and participants,
    19–20, 23, 76, 83, 98–100
  decentralized rulership and, 5–6
  defeat of peasants, 27–29, 137, 145
  demand for godly law and, 17, 21–22,
    76–77, 83–89
  demonstrations and protest marches,
    20–21, 74–82
  Dürer's design for monument of defeat of
    peasants, 141–42
  factors in failure of, 28
  Gaismair's territorial constitution for
    Tirol, 100–105
  importance of "The Twelve Articles,"
    21–22, 76–82
  influence of Reformation on, 3, 16, 21, 55
  initial concessions of lords, 17, 27
  Luther's cautions against violence, 3, 12,
    57–59
  Luther's condemnation of, 3, 26, 27, 106,
    108–11, 112–13, 128–34, 137–40
  main geographic theaters of, 17–19,
    144–45
  map of, 18
  military organization in, 19, 22–24, 93–97
  Müntzer's sanction of active resistance,
    13–14, 69–73, 98–100
  onset and spread of, 6, 15–20, 74, 144
  political localism and, 26
  political organization in, 24–26, 83–92
  refusal to pay dues and tithes, 15, 16, 17,
    78–79
  scope of, 1–3
  secular vs. religious concerns, 16, 19, 21,
    74–75, 76–82, 100–105
  social composition of, 19
  supporters of, 19–20
  treatise arguing legitimacy of rebellion,
    26–27, 113–27

Peasants' War (*cont.*)
 Treaty of Weingarten, 27, 144
 See also Bund (political unions); *Haufens* (bands)
Pfeiffer, Heinrich, 15, 144
political factors
 conflict about authority to institute reform, 12–13, 29–30
 impact of decentralized government, 5–6
 political unions, 24–26
 See also secular authority
political unions. *See Bund* (political unions)
"'Poor Conrad' Movement in Württemberg, The," 40–42, 143
Pope Leo X, 9
 "Arise, O Lord" (*Exsurge domini*), 46–49
prostitution, 24, 54, 94
purgatory doctrine, Luther's attack on, 1, 9, 43–46

Reformation
 Anabaptist dissenters and, 30
 anticlericalism and iconoclasm of, 10–11
 conflict about authority to institute reform, 12–13, 29–30
 discontent and unrest prior to, 3–8, 35–42
 first vernacular liturgy of, 13, 68
 as gospel of social unrest, 10–11
 influence on Peasants' War, 3, 16, 21, 55
 Luther on reform of Christian estate, 50–54
 Luther on rights of the congregation, 13, 65–68
 Luther's initiation of, 1, 8–10, 43–44
 Luther's "Ninety-Five Theses," 43–46
 Luther's opposition to rebellion, 3, 12, 57–59
 Luther's vernacular translation of Bible, 10, 143
 Müntzer's radical reforms, 13–14, 68–73
 oral and visual messages, 12, 14, 55–56, 59–60
 Pope Leo X's response to, 46–49
 rejection of religious authority, 1, 3, 9, 10, 50–53, 67–68
 in urban centers, 11–12
 Zwingli's version of, 13, 61–65
reformation literature
 early reform projects, 7–8, 35
 impact of Ninety-Five Theses, 43–44
 in urban centers, 11–12
republicanism
 commoners' political associations and, 24–25
 Gaismair's territorial constitution, 100–105
 in Luther's communal Reformation, 13, 65–68
 peasant political associations and, 83–92
 of Swiss Confederation, 8, 13, 24, 26, 113, 115

"To the Assembly of the Common Peasantry," 115–27
 in Zwingli's view of Reformation, 13, 61–65
resistance, right of
 Müntzer's view of, 13–14, 69–73, 98–100
 Schappeler's treatise on, 26–27, 113–27
 Zwingli's view of, 13, 61–65
"Rights of a Christian Congregation, The" (Luther), 65–68
Roth, Stephan, Mühlpfort's letter to, 135–37

salvation
 Luther's doctrine of, 8–9
 "pure Word" of God and, 10
Schappeler, Christoph
 on legitimacy of Peasants' War, 26–27
 "The Twelve Articles of the Upper Swabian Peasants," 76–82
 "To the Assembly of the Common Peasantry," 26, 113–27
secular authority
 Luther on ecclesiastical authority of, 12–13, 29–30, 50–54, 61
 Luther on failings of, 53–54, 107–8
 Luther on limitation of ecclesiastic authority of, 13, 65–68
 Müntzer's sanction of active resistance against, 13–14, 69–73, 98–100
 prelates as, 2, 3
 Zwingli on community right to recall, 13, 61–65
 Zwingli's view of powers of, 13, 61–65
 See also territorial principalities
serfdom
 period of relaxed burdens of, 4
 political union demands, 87, 88, 90–92
 popular grievances against, 16, 40–42, 74–75, 78–82
 refusal to pay dues and services, 15, 17, 78–79
 rural communes and, 14
 "The Twelve Articles" and, 22, 78–82
 as violation of Christian principles, 16
"Sermon to the Princes" (Müntzer), 68–73, 144
"Sincere Admonition to Guard against Rebellion, A" (Luther), 57–59
"Sixty-Seven Articles, The" (Zwingli), 13, 61–65, 143
social estates
 Bundschuh and, 24, 35
 reformation literature on, 7
 rejection of clerical privileges, 12, 50–53
socioeconomic factors
 impact of long-term expansion, 4–5
 late medieval downturn, 4
 need for reform and, 3–8
 population increase, 4–5
 in urban reformation, 12
Speyer, *Bundschuh* conspiracy in, 35–38, 143

spice traffic, 53
St. Peter's Basilica, 7
Stühlingen uprising, 15, 16, 74–75, 144
Swabian League, 27, 144
Swiss Confederation
  peasant uprisings and, 8, 36
  political principles of, 24, 26, 113, 115
  Zwingli's reform program in, 13, 61–65

taxation
  by church, 7
  death taxes, 82
  Luther on unjust, 108
  in territorial states, 6, 40, 41
"Territorial Constitution for the Tirol"
  (Gaismair), 100–105, 145
territorial principalities
  Bunds' claims of a *Landschaft* in, 25–26
  with fragmented leadership, 25–26
  origins of peasant uprisings in, 6
  power of rulers of, 5–6, 7
  representative assemblies in, 6, 25, 40
  revenue-enhancing devices in, 6, 40
  See also nobility; secular authority
Tirol rebellion, 28, 100–105, 144
"Title Page of 'Against the Murdering and
  Robbing Hordes of Peasants,'" 128–29
"Title Page of Pamphilus Gegenbach's *The
  Bundschuh*," 38–39
"Title Page of 'The Memmingen Federal
  Ordinance,'" 85–86
"Title Page of 'To the Assembly of the Com-
  mon Peasantry,'" 113–14
"To the Assembly of the Common Peas-
  antry" (Schappeler), 26, 113–27, 144
  title page of, 113–14
"To the Christian Nobility of the German
  Nation" (Luther), 7, 50–54, 143

Treaty of Weingarten, 27, 144
"Twelve Articles of the Upper Swabian
  Peasants, The" (Lotzer, Schappeler),
  21, 22, 76–82, 87, 144
  Luther's response to, 26, 106–13

Ulrich, Duke of Württemberg, 40
Upper Rhine region revolt, 8, 15, 16–17, 144
Upper Swabia rebellion, 6, 17, 27, 76–82

violence
  anticlerical, 11, 19, 24, 36, 37, 57, 59–60
  in defeat of peasants, 27–29
  looting and plundering, 20–21, 24, 36, 37,
    93, 131
  Luther's cautions against use of, 3, 12,
    57–59
  Luther's condemnation of peasant, 26, 27,
    108–11, 112–13, 128–34, 137–40
  Luther's urging princes to, 28–29, 130–34
von Berlichingen, Götz, 19

Waldshut rebellion, 16
Wittenberg, 8, 10, 43
women
  in Peasants' War, 24
  role in popular disturbances, 59
woodlands, grievances about, 41–42, 80
worldly ban, 84, 90–92
Württemberg, peasant uprising in, 40–42

Zurich
  peasant uprising near, 15–16
  reform program in, 13, 61–65, 143
Zwingli, Huldrych, 76
  reform program of, 13, 61–65, 143
  "The Sixty-Seven Articles," 13, 61–65, 143
  Waldshut rebellion and, 16